CRIMINAL INJUSTICE

Violence Against Women in Brazil

An Americas Watch Report

Human Rights Watch

New York · Washington · Los Angeles · London

Printed in the United States of America

Americas Watch

Americas Watch was established in 1981 to monitor and promote the observance of internationally recognized human rights in Latin America and the Caribbean. The chair of Americas Watch is Peter D. Bell and the vice chairs are Stephen L. Kass and Marina Kaufman. Juan E. Méndez is the executive director; Cynthia Arnson and Anne Manuel are the associate directors; David Holliday is the director of San Salvador office; Cynthia Brown is the representative in Santiago; Patricia Pittman is the representative in Buenos Aires; Mary Jane Camejo is the research associate; Clifford C. Rohde and Patricia Sinay are associates.

The Women's Rights Project

The Women's Rights Project of Human Rights Watch was established in 1990 to monitor violence against women and gender discrimination throughout the world. Dorothy Q. Thomas is the director; Michele E. Beasley is a Georgetown University WLPP Fellow and Dionne A. Morris is the associate.

Library of Congress Cataloging-in-Publication Data

Criminal injustice : violence against women in Brazil.
p. cm. – (An Americas Watch report)
Includes bibliographical references.
ISBN 1-56432-048-0 :
1. Women--Brazil--Crimes against. 2. Women's rights--Brazil. 3. Women--Legal status, laws, etc.--Brazil. 4. Violence--Brazil. I. Human Rights Watch (Organization) II. Series.
HV6250.4.W65C76 1991
362.88'082--dc20

91-39040
CIP

CONTENTS

ACKNOWLEDGEMENTS

This report was written by Dorothy Q. Thomas, Director of the Women's Rights Project of Human Rights Watch, edited by Ken Roth, Deputy Director of Human Rights Watch and proofread by Michele E. Beasley and Dionne A. Morris, who also provided production assistance.

Americas Watch gratefully acknowledges the many individuals and organizations in the United States and Brazil without whom this report would not have been possible. In particular, we would like to thank Silvia Pimentel, Jacqueline Pitanguy, the Núcleo de Estudos da Violência or Center for the Study of Violence at the University of São Paulo and all the women police officers, human rights monitors, lawyers, activists (including Cemina and Viva Mulher) and the victims of domestic violence and their families in Brazil who helped us understand events there. We are grateful for research and logistical assistance to Tana Silva and for translation to Helena Vieira and Debra J. Herring.

On August 5, 1988, in the Brazilian city of Apucarana, João Lopes (nicknamed "Joe Slick"), after spending two days in search of his wife, Terezinha Ribeiro Lopes, arrived at a hotel where he believed her to be with her lover, José Gaspar Felix. A bellman took him to the room of the two people answering to their description. At the bellman's request, the door was opened by José Felix who, with no forewarning, was stabbed repeatedly in the chest by João Lopes. Lopes then ran after his wife, who fled naked from the room and out of the hotel. Lopes chased his wife into the streets and caught up to her at the door of a hospital where he killed her with two knife wounds.

The all-male jury[1] *accepted the argument advanced by the defense that Lopes had acted in legitimate defense of his offended honor in killing the two victims and unanimously absolved him of the double homicide. The state appellate court in Paraná upheld this decision.*

The Federal Public Ministry responsible for prosecuting the case sought recourse to the Superior Tribunal of Justice, Brazil's highest court of appeal. The Tribunal accepted the prosecution's appeal,[2] *and on March 11, 1991 overturned the lower court's decision and ordered a new trial. In so doing, the Tribunal declared that murder cannot be conceived of as a legitimate response to adultery and that what is being defended in this type of crime is not honor, but "self-esteem, vanity and the pride of the Lord who sees his wife as property."*[3]

The Superior Tribunal's decision represented an historic moment, both for the Brazilian judiciary and for the feminist activists who waged a twenty-year campaign against the honor defense and the proprietary attitudes towards women on which it is based. However, despite such welcome progress, the reality is that in Brazil – as elsewhere – wife-murder is still considered an appropriate response to alleged unfaithfulness. On August 29, the Lopes case was re-tried in the State Court of Paraná, and Lopes was again acquitted of the double homicide on the grounds of legitimate defense of honor. The decision perpetuates a culture of impunity in wife-murder crimes sanctioned by the Brazilian

---

[1] Not all jurors in Brazil are male. The defense attorney in the *Lopes* case felt the sex of the jurors had "nothing to do" with the decision. He chose two women jurors for the trial, but they were rejected by the prosecution.

[2] Under Brazilian law prosecutors have a right to appeal an acquittal when the decision is made against all available facts in the case.

[3] Decision of the Superior Tribunal de Justiça, March 11, 1991, Brasilia.

courts and represents a victory of social prejudice over the rule of law in Brazil.

I. INTRODUCTION

In April of this year, Americas Watch, together with the Women's Rights Project of Human Rights Watch, travelled to Brazil to assess the response of the Brazilian government to the problem of domestic violence. This report contains the findings of that mission. It focuses on wife-murder, domestic battery and rape. It constitutes the first report of the newly formed Women's Rights Project of Human Rights Watch which monitors violence against women and discrimination on the basis of sex throughout the world.

The crime of domestic violence is not unique to Brazil. According to recent United Nations reports, it exists in all regions, classes and cultures.[4] Women all over the world and from all walks of life are at risk from violence in the home, usually at the hands of their husband or lover. Although the exact number of abused women will probably never be known,[5] available information indicates unequivocally that domestic violence is a common and serious problem in developed and developing countries alike.[6]

Although domestic violence is common and widespread, it has traditionally been perceived as a private, family problem, beyond the scope of state responsibility. Indeed, in the past husbands have had the legal right to punish or even kill their wives with impunity.[7] Only

---

[4] *The World's Women 1970–1990: Trends and Statistics*, United Nations (New York, 1991), p. 19.

[5] Attempts to quantify levels of domestic abuse are hampered by, among other things, a lack of available and accurate statistics and case work and a disinclination of women to report domestic-abuse crimes.

[6] Statistics compiled for 1990 by the U.S. National Coalition Against Domestic Violence indicate that 30% of all female homicides in the United States take place in the home at the hands of a husband or lover.

[7] Connors, Jane Frances, *Violence Against Women in the Family*, United Nations (New York:1989), p. 11. Connors cites Blackstone's 1775 *Commentaries on the Laws of England* which stated that a husband was empowered to correct his wife "in the same moderation that a man is allowed to correct his apprentice or children." She also found that this power "was confirmed in judicial decisions in England and North America, where domestic chastisement of the wife went unpunished unless some permanent injury

gradually changing social attitudes and increased reporting have propelled the problem into the public eye. And as the nature and severity of violence in the home has become evident, so has the responsibility of governments to prosecute such abuse as they would any other violent crime.

The Women's Rights Project chose to issue its first report on domestic violence and state responsibility in Brazil because of the severity of Brazil's domestic violence problem, made visible largely by the campaigning of the women's movement, and the degree to which such abuse continues to receive both the explicit and implicit sanction of the Brazilian government.[8] Our report focuses on the problem of impunity, as reflected primarily in the use of the honor defense to exculpate men accused of killing their wives. It also examines the more general failure of the Brazilian criminal justice system to investigate and prosecute in a non–discriminatory manner crimes of domestic violence against women, in contravention of Brazil's obligations under international law.

* * * * * *

For over twenty years, the Brazilian women's movement has actively campaigned against domestic violence and the failure of the Brazilian government to adequately punish such abuse. As a result of their efforts, domestic violence emerged in the early 1980s as a major public policy issue, and councils on women were integrated into state and federal administrations. The year 1984 saw the ratification by Brazil of the Convention on the Elimination of All Forms of Discrimination Against Women (CEDAW) followed by the creation of specialized police stations staffed by female officers to deal exclusively with crimes of violence

---

or death resulted. Even where permanent injury or death resulted, the husband's actions were often justified on the grounds of, for example, provocation, and the penalty was always light. The husband's right to chastise his wife received acceptance in popular culture by being known as "the rule of thumb," because it appeared that normal wife–beating involved chastisement with a stick no bigger than a man's thumb."

[8] Prior Americas Watch reports and newsletters on Brazil are: Police Abuse in Brazil: *Police Abuse in Brazil: Summary Exections in São Paulo and Rio de Janeiro*, December 1987 (New York: Americas Watch, 1987); *Prison Conditions in Brazil*, April 1989 (New York: Americas Watch, 1989); *News from Americas Watch*, "Notorious Jail Operating in São Paulo," October 1989; *News from Americas Watch*, "On Trial in Brazil: Rural Violence and the Murder of Chico Mendes," December 1990; *News from Americas Watch*, "Forced Labor in Brazil," December 1990; *Rural Violence in Brazil*, February 1991 (New York: Americas Watch, 1991).

against women in 1985. A nationwide women's rights campaign during the drafting of the 1988 Constitution led to constitutional guarantees of equality before the law and established an obligation by the government to prevent violence in the home.

Despite these welcome developments, which culminated in the Superior Tribunal's rejection of the legitimate defense of honor in *Lopes*, domestic violence continues to increase and the response of the Brazilian government and its public institutions to this serious problem remains woefully inadequate.

Although national homicide statistics broken down by gender are not available, existing information indicates that wife–murder is a common crime. A 1991 study of more than 6,000 violent crimes against Brazilian women from 1987 to 1989 found that 400 incidents involved murders of women by their husbands or lovers.[9]

It is still possible in Brazil for a man to kill his allegedly unfaithful wife and be absolved on the grounds of honor, particularly in Brazil's interior, where one state prosecutor told Americas Watch the honor defense is successful 80 percent of the time. The notion of "provocation by the victim" continues to result in unduly short prison terms for wife–murder, even in cases involving premeditation. Moreover, such crimes are often reclassified as less serious charges, and defendants, who are usually first time offenders, receive preferential treatment from the courts despite the extreme gravity of their crime.

Available statistics show that over 70 percent of all reported incidents of violence against women in Brazil take place in the home. In almost all of these cases the abuser was either the woman's husband or her lover. Over 40 percent involved serious bodily injury caused by, among other things, punching, slapping, kicking, tying up and spanking, burning of the breasts and genitals, and strangulation.

Physical and sexual abuse in the home has become more visible and is more often investigated as a result of the women's police stations. But these stations have been severely hampered in their efforts by shifting and often diminishing government support, most clearly reflected in their limited distribution throughout the country (a total of 74 of which 50 are concentrated in the state of São Paulo alone), under–staffing and a lack of specialized training for the officers. In part because of these difficulties, the police often fail to classify domestic abuse as a crime, or

---

[9] Letícia Lins, *Jornal do Brasil*, April 1, 1991. The article cites a study prepared by Viva Mulher!, a group based in the northeastern capitol of Recife which monitors crimes of violence against women.

classify domestic abuse crimes too leniently, and discriminatory attitudes towards female victims persist.

Moreover, female victims still have little reason to expect that their abusers – once denounced – will ever be punished. A police chief in Rio de Janeiro told Americas Watch that to her knowledge, of more than 2,000 battery and sexual assault cases registered at her station in 1990, not a single one had ended in punishment of the accused. The São Luis women's police station in the northeastern state of Maranhão reported that of over 4,000 cases of physical and sexual assault registered with the station, only 300 were ever forwarded for processing and only two yielded punishment for the accused.

Brazil's criminal law is part of the problem. In the Brazilian Penal Code, rape is defined as a crime against custom rather than a crime against an individual person -- society rather than the female victim is the offended party. Most other sex crimes are deemed crimes only if the victim is a "virgin" or "honest" woman. If a woman does not fit this "customary" stereotype, she is likely to be accused of having consented to the crime and it is unlikely to be investigated. Moreover, pursuit of these cases by law depends on the initiative of the victim, not the state; if at anytime she desists from prosecution the case will be dropped. Of over 800 cases of rape reported to the São Paulo women's police stations from 1985 to 1989, less than 1/4 were ever investigated.

Marital rape, in particular, is severely under-reported and least likely to be prosecuted. While marital rape theoretically is included within the general prohibition against rape, in practice it is not commonly viewed by the courts as a crime. Under the Brazilian Civil Code, the refusal of sexual relations is cause for legal separation. According to several attorneys with whom Americas Watch spoke, when a husband uses violence to compel his wife to have sexual relations, it is viewed by the courts as enforcing the wife's conjugal obligations, not as rape. As a result, rape in the home, with the exception of incest, is almost never punished.

It is mandated by law that a victim of sexual or physical abuse be examined by the Medical-Legal Institute (IML), which has sole jurisdiction over the medical analysis of all crimes of physical or sexual violence as defined under Brazilian law. Yet, the IMLs are concentrated in urban areas, often in obscure locations and they are understaffed, with few female doctors, and none of the staff has specialized training in sexual abuse crimes. Examiners have been found to omit medical-legal information which is crucial to proving the existence of the crime.

Women's rights activists and legal scholars are seeking changes in the medical-legal system and Civil and Penal Code reforms[10] which would, among other things, equalize women's status in the home, transform rape into a crime against a person rather than custom, and eliminate all reference to "honest" or "virgin" victims in the definition of other sex crimes. These reforms, which follow from the 1988 Constitution, are stalled in the National Assembly, leaving Brazilian women in the precarious state of having constitutional rights which are not reflected in the codes designed to enforce those rights.

* * * * * *

Under international law, the Brazilian government has an obligation to guarantee civil and political rights and to guarantee equality before the law and equal protection of the law for all its citizens, without regard to gender. Article 3 of the International Covenant on Civil and Political Rights provides for "the equal right of men and women to the enjoyment of all civil and political rights...." Article 26 further provides that "all persons are equal before the law and are entitled without any discrimination to the equal protection of the law." Furthermore, the Convention on the Elimination of all Forms of Discrimination Against Women (CEDAW), which Brazil ratified in 1984, obligates state parties "to pursue a policy of eliminating discrimination...to refrain from engaging in any act of discrimination...[and] to ensure that public authorities and institutions shall act in conformity with this obligation."

The continued application of the honor defense which has no basis in law, is inherently biased, and is almost exclusively applied to wife-murder; the emphasis on "provocation" by the victim even in pre-meditated wife-murder crimes; the near total failure to prosecute battery and rape in the home; and the prejudicial treatment of rape victims both in law and in fact, establish a pattern of discriminatory treatment by the criminal justice system of female victims of domestic violence. Because of this pattern we believe that Brazil is failing to meet its international obligations to guarantee to its female citizens the equal enjoyment of their civil and political rights and the equal protection of the law.

There should be no doubt about the capacity of the Brazilian government to meet these obligations. The Superior Tribunal's decision

---

[10] The women's movement first introduced Civil Code reforms in 1981. Since that time, the proposed reforms have been rewritten eight times in different proposals by several congresspeople and the Ministry of Justice. No final proposal has been adopted. Penal Code reforms were presented to the Congress in March 1991.

in *Lopes*, the 1988 Constitution and the creation of women's police stations reveal the existence of adequate legal and institutional structures. What is lacking is the political will to implement these obligations fully and fairly. As a result, female victims of domestic violence in Brazil cannot reasonably expect to obtain consistently fair treatment from the criminal justice system.

II. BACKGROUND

A. The Role of the Women's Movement

The Superior Tribunal's rejection of the honor defense in *Lopes* follows a decade–long struggle of Brazilian feminists to de–legitimate the "legitimate defense of honor" and to force the state to prosecute wife–murder and other domestic violence crimes to the full extent of the law. This effort began in connection with two famous cases in Rio de Janeiro and São Paulo.

The first involved Raul Doca Street who in 1979 murdered his lover after she decided to break off their relationship. During Street's first trial the defense argued he had acted in legitimate defense of his offended honor. While the court ultimately did not accept the honor defense, it did accept the notion that Street acted in a moment of "violent emotion" (discussed below), which it took as a mitigating factor justifying a sentence of only two years for the crime. The decision was appealed and at Street's second trial in 1980, thousands of women gathered outside the courthouse protesting the earlier decision. Street ultimately was sentenced to fifteen years in prison – the standard sentence for intentional homicide.

The second case, which took place in 1981, involved Lindomar Castilho, a famous Brazilian singer who shot his wife, Eliane, and her cousin, who Lindomar believed was Eliane's lover. Eliane died but her cousin survived. In the pre–trial phase, the defense argued that the crime had been motivated by "violent emotion due to the unjust provocation of the victim," whereas the prosecution charged that the crime was premeditated and that Eliane's active nightlife and love relationship were "not valid reasons for a crime of this magnitude." The judge ultimately accepted violent emotion as a factor in the crime. Women's rights activists immediately protested the judge's ruling. In 1984, when the case was finally brought to trial, the jury rejected the "violent emotion" defense and Lindomar was sentenced to 12 years in prison.

These two cases, together with two similar cases heard at the time in Minas Gerais, galvanized a national women's movement to protest domestic violence and the inadequate, often discriminatory response of the Brazilian police and judiciary.

This movement against domestic violence emerged, in part, against the background of Brazil's military dictatorship and in the context of the gradual liberalization which began in the late 1970s and culminated in the 1985 indirect election of a civilian president and the creation of the new Brazilian Republic. Reports on sexual abuse, torture and murder of political prisoners during the dictatorship led to a national debate about violence and, in the mid-1970s, to the creation of a number of non-governmental human rights organizations in which women were very active.

With the development of the broadly based pro-democracy movement, "the debate on violence enlarged to include many forms of its exercise, besides those which occurred directly at the hands of the authoritarian state."[11] Women's organizations proliferated during this period,[12] particularly SOS-Mulher, a nationwide organization devoted to combatting violence against women. As a result of these developments, gender-specific issues which had previously been considered "private" or "personal," such as domestic violence, emerged as major public policy concerns.

Active women in both urban and rural areas and across racial and economic divides seized on domestic violence and used it successfully to propel gender concerns into the broader public policy debate. A series of local demonstrations led to several nationwide protests against domestic violence from which emerged the anonymous slogan that became the crie de coeur of the Brazilian women's movement: "Those who love don't kill."

The 1982 elections, which represented the first direct balloting for state governor since 1965,[13] demonstrated the emergence of the women's movement as a major political force. Women were very active during the campaign, and gender-specific demands were for the first time integrated into the platforms of the various political parties. As a result of the 1982 elections several opposition candidates won state governorships, most notably in São Paulo and Rio de Janeiro. Women's demands were soon institutionalized in these states through the creation of state councils of women.

The first state council (*Conselho Estadual da Condição Feminina*) was created in São Paulo in 1983. Its primary goals were to increase women's access to the policy-making process and to promote women's

---

[11] Jacqueline Pitanguy, former president National Council of Women's Rights, "Violence Against Women: Addressing a Global Problem," report to the Ford Foundation, 1991, p. 2 (mimeo).

[12] Sonia Alvarez writing in *Democratizing Brazil*, edited by Alfred Stepan, (Oxford, 1989), p. 211, notes the "presence of over 400 feminist groups in the major Brazilian urban centers" in the mid-1970s.

[13] Skidmore, Thomas E., in *Democratizing Brazil*, p. 23.

interests within the state administration. It was followed by the creation of similar councils in many other states and, in 1985, under the auspices of the first civilian President, Tancredo Neves, by the creation of a National Council for Women's Rights (CNDM), one of the very few things Neves did during his brief tenure as President which was cut short by his death in March of that year. The CNDM was a federal body "in charge of designing and developing public policy to improve the condition of women."[14]

A major goal of both the state and national councils was combatting violence against women. CNDM president Jacqueline Pitanguy put gender-specific violence at the top of the Council's political agenda, launching a "say no to violence against women" campaign and compiling several documents detailing violence against women and criticizing the inadequate penal and judicial response.

During this period, women also began to be better represented in professional and political life. According to research conducted in 1984, "the female economically active population (EAP) went from 18.5 percent in 1970 to 26.9 percent in 1980, a proportion which accounts for 41 percent of the increase in the total EAP over the decade."[15]

The type of women's employment also changed. "The share of female EAP increased in administrative occupations (from 8.2 percent in 1960 to 15.4 percent in 1980) and in professions of higher prestige (engineers, architects, doctors, dentists, economists, university professors and lawyers which went from 19,000 in 1970 to 95,800 in 1980)."[16] In 1980, the number of women enrolled in Brazilian universities almost equaled the number of men.[17] According to statistics compiled by the Inter-American Commission on Women, women now represent 52 percent of Brazil's voting population.[18]

---

[14] Pitanguy, p. 2.

[15] Boschi, Renato Paul, "The Art of Associating: Social Movements, the Middle Class and Grassroots Politics in urban Brazil," Final Report for the Tinker Foundation, December 1984, quoted in Sonia Alvarez, "Politicizing Gender and Engendering Democracy" in *Democratizing Brazil*, p. 211.

[16] Ibid., p. 211.

[17] Ibid., p. 211.

[18] Comissão Interamericana de Mulheres, Brazil report, July 1990.

Women's increased economic and political power coupled with the development of autonomous and state-affiliated women's institutions, enabled the women's movement to press for fundamental changes in the state's response to gender-specific violence. In 1985, women's groups, together with the state council on women, persuaded São Paulo's opposition party mayor to establish a woman's police station, staffed entirely by women and dedicated solely to crimes of violence against women, excluding homicide, which was not viewed as a gender-specific crime.[19] By late 1985, eight women's police stations (*Delegacias De Defesa Da Mulher*, hereafter *delegacias*) had opened in the state of São Paulo, and by 1990 there were 74 throughout the country.[20]

The women's *delegacias* represented an integrated approach to the problem of domestic violence. They were designed to investigate gender-specific crimes, and to provide psychological and legal counseling. The female police officers (*delegadas*) were to receive training in all aspects of domestic violence, from its psychological impact to the legal remedies available to the victim. The medical practitioners at the Medical Legal Institute (IML), charged with certifying the nature of physical injuries to the police, were also to receive such training. Finally, the *delegacias* were to integrate perspectives gained in their work into the activities of the other stations and, in some states, a permanent commission was formed to ensure these objectives were met.

By the mid-1980s, the now active and institutionalized women's movement began to focus on legal reform to consolidate their hard-won gains. Women were granted the franchise in 1932, but until a 1962 Civil Code reform they were considered perpetual subordinates, legally equated with "minors, spendthrifts and backwoodsmen"[21] and could not, for example, work outside the home without their husbands' consent.[22] The

---

[19] In general, the *delegacias*' responsibilities include crimes involving bodily wounds, threats, and sexual crimes, including rape.

[20] Pitanguy, Jacqueline, "Violence Against Women: A Global Problem," report to the Ford Foundation, 1991.

[21] de Fonseca, Romy Medeiros, "Law and the Condition of Women in Brazil," cited in *Law and the Status of Women*, Columbia Human Rights Review, (New York: 1977), p. 14.

[22] Lombardi, Karen, "Retrato da Mulher Brasileira," 1990 (mimeo).

reform equalized women's legal status, but still left the male as the head of the family unit.[23]

In 1984, women's rights advocates secured Brazil's adoption of the Convention on the Elimination of All Forms of Discrimination Against Women (CEDAW), although with several reservations.[24] In 1986, the women's movement held a national constitutional forum to draft a list of recommendations for consideration by the Constituent Assembly, which was elected in the 1986 congressional elections to take up the task of writing a new Brazilian Constitution. They sought, among other things, equality before and equal protection of the law, the same rights and responsibilities as men, and equal opportunity in health, education, employment and civil status. They also called on the Assembly to obligate the state to take measures to counter violence in the home. Their proposal to the Assembly stated:

> All are equal before the law which will punish any discrimination which threatens human rights. No one will be prejudiced or privileged on the basis of place of birth, race, color, sex....The public authorities, through specific programs, will promote social, political, economic and educational equality.[25]

---

[23] de Fonseca, p. 16.

[24] Brazil entered reservations regarding the sections of the Convention that guarantee the equal rights of men and women to choose their residence and domicile, to have equal rights to enter into marriage, during marriage and at its dissolution, and to have the same personal rights, including the right to choose a family name. Brazil also entered reservations to the Convention article according the same rights "for both spouses in respect of ownership, acquisition, management, administration, enjoyment and disposition of property...."

International legal scholar Rebecca Cook notes that "though over one hundred countries have joined the convention, 21 of these countries, including Brazil, have filed over a total of 80 reservations to the Convention by which they limit their obligations. In contrast, 123 countries have joined the International Convention on all Forms of Racial Discrimination and only two countries have reserved certain of their obligations to eliminate racial discrimination," cited in "Reservations to the Convention on the Elimination of All Forms of Discrimination Against Women," Virginia Journal of International Law, Vol. 30, No. 2, Spring 1990.

[25] CNDM, "Quadro Comparativo dos Direitos da Mulher na Constituinte," July 1988 (mimeo), cited in Alvarez, p. 251.

The new Constitution, enacted in 1988, reflects many of the national women's movement's demands.[26] In particular, Article 226, Paragraph 8 provides that "the state should assist the family, in the person of each of its members, and should create mechanisms so as to impede violence in the sphere of its relationships." Similar provisions have been adopted in state constitutions throughout Brazil.

The achievements of the Brazilian women's movement in bolstering the state's response to domestic violence have been impressive. From 1980 to 1990 a national women's movement committed to combatting violence emerged, entered the political arena, created state and federal agencies to improve the state's response to violence in the home, and secured far-reaching legal reforms. In the six years since the birth of the new republic, the autonomous women's movement, though divided by racial and class differences, has on account of these same differences expanded its popular base and continues to organize actively for fundamental civil, political, economic and social reforms.

Yet, there is still a long way to go. Changes in political and economic power since the onset of the new republic have diminished the scope and effectiveness of initiatives launched in the euphoria of the early years. New state and federal administrations less sympathetic to gender-specific concerns have limited the ability of state-affiliated women's agencies, like the state and national councils of women, to consolidate their gains and push for further reforms.[27] Even the *delegacias* of women, while still recognized as major improvements in the police response to violence against women, have suffered from diminishing government support which has curtailed their effectiveness and growth.

The passage of Civil and Penal Code reforms pursuant to the Constitution have been stalled in the Assembly for some time and, despite continued mobilization by the women's movement, the Brazilian government has failed to meet its international obligation to report to the

---

[26] Women's rights advocates secured, for example, maternity and paternity leave, improved prison conditions for women, and improved labor and health standards. However, their efforts to decriminalize abortion failed. Abortion is currently illegal in Brazil, except in cases of rape or risk to maternal health.

[27] Former president of the National Council for Women's Rights Jacqueline Pitanguy notes that in 1989 just such a "serious political crisis weakened the organ." Pitanguy, Jacqueline, "Violence Against Women: Addressing a Global Problem," Report to the Ford Foundation, 1991.

UN committee which oversees the Convention on the Elimination of All Forms of Discrimination against Women (CEDAW).

In the meantime, as the following section documents, domestic violence continues to increase.

B. Domestic Violence: Statistical Evidence

Brazil's 1988 census, conducted by the Brazilian Institute for Geography and Statistics (IBGE), includes the first national statistics by gender on crimes of physical abuse and the extent to which they are reported to the police and prosecuted in the courts. The statistics show that Brazil has a serious and mounting problem of domestic violence.

The IBGE study found that from October 1987 to September 1988, 1,153,300 people declared to the IBGE that they had been victims of physical abuse. Of these, the vast majority of the victims lived in urban areas.[28] Sixty percent of the victims were men and forty percent were women. A marked difference emerged in the nature of violence suffered by women as opposed to men. For Brazilian men, murder and physical abuse primarily involve acquaintances or strangers and occur outside the home. For Brazilian women, the opposite is true. The 1988 census showed that men were abused by relatives (including spouses) only ten percent of the time, while women are related to their abuser in over half of the cases of reported physical violence.

The national IBGE study confirms similar, and even more disturbing trends in state studies of domestic abuse reported to the *delegacias* of women. For example, a 1987 study of over 2,000 battery cases registered at the São Paulo *delegacia* from August to December 1985 found that over seventy percent of all reported crimes of violence against women occurred in the home. Of these, the vast majority took place between couples who had been living together for periods of three to nine years. Seventy five percent of the abusers were legally married to the victim, and the remainder were live-in lovers. (The study found no difference in behavior between these two sub-groups.)

A chilling picture of domestic tyranny emerges from these studies and the many individuals with whom we spoke. Most women who fall victim to physical abuse can expect to experience such violence in their own home by their spouse or lover. Well over a third of domestic violence will involve serious injury, usually committed by the aggressor's feet and

---

[28] Women's rights activists interviewed by Americas Watch stressed that higher reporting rates in the cities reflects in part the concentration of the women's movement in urban areas rather than outlying rural communities.

fists. Examples of physical abuse cited in a 1989 study of violence against women in the state of Pernambuco included beating, tying up and spanking, burning the genitals and breasts with cigarettes, strangulation, inserting objects in the victim's vagina (such as bottles and pieces of wood) and throwing alcohol and fire on the victim.[29] The study also noted repeated physical abuse of pregnant women in which the aggressors "aimed for the womb, breasts and vagina."[30]

After battery and serious threat of death or physical harm, rape is the third most reported form of violence against women, although by all accounts the "under registration of sexual occurrences is significant."[31] Of those cases that are reported, rape appears to occur less frequently in the domestic context than it does outside the home. A study of reported rapes in the state of Minas Gerias found that over half were perpetrated by strangers.[32] However, researchers were quick to point out that these limited statistics do not support the conclusion that marital rape does not frequently occur. They stressed that prevailing attitudes that marital rape is not a crime (see section on rape, discussed below) may substantially reduce both reporting and investigation.

Neither the census nor the various police studies examine the incidence of homicide in which females are victim. Such crimes are handled by special police stations which deal exclusively with this type of offense and which do not provide murder statistics broken down according to gender. In addition, the number of homicides in which females are victims is difficult to determine accurately because they are often unreported, particularly in the poorer or more remote areas of the country.[33]

---

[29] *Jornal do Commercio*, April 28, 1990.

[30] Ibid. The 1987 São Paulo study also detailed repeated incidents of abuse of pregnant women. The study cites research indicating that pregnancy is one possible catalyst for physical abuse, but the sample was not large enough to draw any broad conclusions in this regard.

[31] Fundação SEADE, Conselho Estadual Da Condição Feminina, *Um Retrato Da Violência Contra A Mulher*, (CIP International, 1987).

[32] da Conceição Marques Rubinger, Maria, et al, *Crimes Contra A Mulher: A Violência Denunciada*, (provisional title) forthcoming report prepared with funding from the Ford Foundation, 1991, table 17.

[33] According to interviews conducted by Americas Watch, wife-murders go unreported largely because they happen "behind closed doors." An October 30, 1990

However, according to the University of São Paulo's Center for the Study of Violence, a study of press reports concerning over 3,000 homicides between 1946 and 1988, indicates that wife-murder is a common occurrence. A separate study conducted in the northeastern state of Pernambuco found that of 6,000 reported violent crimes against women between 1987 and 1989, 400 involved women who were murdered by their husbands or lovers.[34] According to the Center's research, of all homicides involving both male and female victims in the home, men kill women with far greater frequency than women kill men.[35]

In the past, particularly prior to the creation of the women's *delegacias*, the incidence and nature of wife-murder, battery and rape were hidden and, as a result, went largely unpunished. As one researcher told Americas Watch, "we knew that the violence against women occurred, but the regular *delegacias* didn't treat women, so no data existed."[36] Now, with the various police studies and the recent census, enough data exists to reveal a drastic and widespread social phenomenon.

However, even as reporting of violence against women in the home has increased and public awareness of its existence intensified, the response of the criminal justice system has been less encouraging. Analysts with whom Americas Watch spoke stressed the continuing failure of Brazil's criminal justice system to treat violence against women as a crime, deserving of investigation and prosection with the same vigor as homicide and physical abuse occurring in the general population.

The following sections discuss the criminal justice system's susceptibility to prejudicial attitudes and review its failure to respond adequately to crimes of violence against women which occur in the home. We look first at wife-murder cases and the use of the legitimate defense of honor – an extra-legal defense which is almost exclusively applied in

---

Miami Herald article also notes that Brazil's "vast territory often shrouds many killings in impunity" and quotes the former president of the national council of women saying that "nobody has any idea how many women are being killed in Rio's slums."

[34] Letícia Lins, *Jornal do Brasil*, April 1, 1991. The article cites a study by the Recife-based Viva Mulher, a non-governmental group which monitors violence against women.

[35] Sam Dillon, *Miami Herald*, October 30, 1990.

[36] Cida Medrado, interview with Americas Watch, April 1991.

homicides involving a female victim and which, as the majority in *Lopes* pointed out, is rooted in attitudes inherently prejudicial to women.

In addition, we examine the defense based on "violent emotion due to the unjust provocation of the victim," commonly known as privileged homicide. While privileged homicide is technically different from the legitimate defense of honor, it often acts as the honor defense's subtle equivalent, resulting in mitigation of sentence in wife–murder cases even when there is strong evidence of premeditation.

III. WIFE-MURDER[37]

A. The Legal Context

Under Brazilian law, homicide is defined as a crime against life (*crime contra a vida*). It is the only crime which requires a jury trial. The Penal Code, passed in 1940, differentiates between unintentional murder (*homicídio culposo*) and intentional murder (*homicídio doloso*). In cases of intentional murder, Article 121 of the code makes a distinction between simple homicide (*homicídio simples*) which carries a penalty of 6 – 20 years and qualified homicide (*homicídio qualificado*) which carries a penalty of 12 – 30 years.

A qualified homicide involves aggravating factors such as a spousal relationship between the aggressor and the victim. Aggravating factors under Article 121, Section 2 of the Penal Code include a base (*torpe*) motive (i.e., one which causes general repugnance, like a murder for money or pleasure), a futile (*fútil*) motive (i.e., one which is so insignificant that it does not constitute an acceptable explanation for the crime), the use of insidious or cruel means, or the use of actions, like a surprise attack, which prevent the victim from defending him or her self.

Article 121, Section 1 of the Penal Code describes attenuating circumstances which can result in the reduction of penalties (*diminuição de pena*) by up to one-third. These include, among other things, being under the influence of violent emotion (*violenta emoção*) caused by an unjust provocation by the victim (*injusta provocação da vítima*).[38] Murders to which this reduction are applied are known as "privileged homicides" and carry an optional sentence of 1 – 6 years.

A homicide is not considered a crime in Brazil if, among other things, it was committed in legitimate self-defense (*legítima defesa*). Under Article 25 of the Penal Code, self-defense is defined as "the case of one

---

[37] We include in this chapter a discussion of both homicides and attempted homicides as well as cases in which the female victim is not the wife but the live-in lover of the accused. Statistics usually separate these two groups but show little differentiation of behavior between them.

[38] Article 28 of the Brazilian Penal Code says that "emotion or passion does not exclude anyone from penal responsibility." However, one Brazilian sociologist has pointed out that the committee in charge of reviewing the Penal Code took a somewhat lenient attitude towards crimes of passion. That is why passion is included as an attenuating circumstance in the articles concerning homicide.

who using the necessary means with moderation reacts against unjust aggression present or imminent to his right or someone else's."

In wife-murder cases the prosecution usually claims that the killing was an intentional homicide, while the defense characterizes it as an unintentional or "privileged homicide." In legitimate defense of honor cases, in which the defense seeks to obtain acquittal for the crime, the defense of honor is equated with legitimate self-defense.

Charges in homicide cases are brought by the prosecutor (*Promotor*) who is under the jurisdiction of the state Attorney General (*Procurador Geral*), who is head of the Public Ministry (*Ministério Público*). Following receipt of the police report, the prosecutor conducts his own investigation and makes his recommendation to the judge regarding whether or not to try the suspect and on what charge. The victim or her family may retain independent counsel to accompany the prosecution during this phase. This attorney does not have the same authority as the prosecutor, but can assist in the gathering of evidence and in questioning, though not subpoenaing, witnesses.

During the pre-trial phase, which begins once the judge receives the prosecutor's recommendation, the judge hears the accused and witnesses on both sides and may subpoena additional witnesses or seek additional evidence. There is no grand jury. The judge alone determines whether there is sufficient evidence for a jury trial for homicide or attempted homicide -- the only crimes in Brazil which merit a jury trial.

After hearing the arguments of both the prosecution and defense and reading the testimony of witnesses, the jury makes its final decision based on answers to a series of questions posed by the judge at the behest of the opposing sides. The questions follow a standard format, although their content reflects the specific facts of the case. The jurors only answer "yes" or "no." They do not consult with one another and convey their answers by secret ballot. Under Article 5 of the Brazilian

Constitution, the sovereignty of the jury's decision is guaranteed.[39] The judge determines the sentence based on the jury's verdict.

B. The Honor Defense

History

Prior to Brazil's independence in 1822, Portuguese colonial law allowed a man who caught his wife in the act of adultery to kill her and her lover, although the reverse was not true.[40] Brazil's first post-independence Penal Code was enacted in 1830 and did away with this rule. However, the popular notion that a man could legitimately kill his adulterous wife persisted. Reinforcing that view is that adultery remains a crime in Brazil today.[41]

Brazil's second Penal Code, enacted in 1890, included an exemption from criminal responsibility for those who committed a crime "under a state of total perturbation of the senses and intelligence." Wife-murder cases soon came to be defended as "crimes of passion" in which the wife's adulterous behavior occasioned such strong emotion in the accused that he experienced a kind of "momentary insanity" resulting in the crime. The emphasis in such cases was placed not on the nature of the crime itself, but on the degree to which the husband intended to commit it.

For the next fifty years, defense attorneys successfully used the "crime of passion" argument to obtain acquittal of husbands accused of

---

[39] Article 5, section 38 of the Brazilian Constitution states "the institution of the jury is recognized in such forms as may be organized by law the following being assured (a) full defense; (b) confidentiality of the balloting; (c) sovereignty of the verdicts; and (d) jurisdiction to try felonious crimes against life."

The Jury Tribunal, commonly known as the popular jury, was first instituted in Brazil in 1822 and has seen several changes in composition and jurisdiction since. At present, state pools of between 300 and 500 potential jurors are chosen each year. Every three months 21 names are chosen by the judge from this larger group, of which seven become the sentencing council. Jury trials continue until a verdict is reached; they are not adjourned.

[40] Corrêa, Mariza, *Os Crimes Da Paixão*, Editora Brasiliense (São Paulo, 1981).

[41] de Fonseca, Dr. Romy Medeiros, "Law and the Condition of Women in Brazil," cited in *Law and the Status of Women*, (Center for Social Development and Humanitarian Affairs, United Nations, NY: 1977) edited by Columbia Human Rights Law Review, p. 23. Penal Code reforms proposed by the women's movement in 1989 suggested eliminating the crime of adultery from Brazilian law.

murdering their wives and, on occasion, though far less frequently, of wives accused of murdering their husbands.[42] It proved so effective in obtaining acquittal that Brazil's third Penal Code, which remains in force today, explicitly states that "emotion or passion does not exclude criminal responsibility."[43] Mental retardation or inability to understand the criminality of an act can eliminate responsibility for a crime, but passion or "violent" emotion can only serve to mitigate sentence.

As a result of this change in the Penal Code, acquittal in wife-murder cases became more difficult to obtain. Defense attorneys, unhappy with this development, devised the legitimate defense of honor as a new exculpatory strategy. Like the "crime of passion" argument, the honor defense shifts attention from the killing itself to the absence of intent on the part of the murderer. However, rather than focusing on the accused's "momentary insanity" as vitiating criminal intent, the honor defense characterizes the accused as having acted spontaneously in legitimate self-defense against an imminent aggression, though against his honor rather than his physical being.

As noted, legitimate self-defense is defined in Brazil as "the case of one who using the necessary means with moderation reacts against unjust aggression present or imminent to his right or someone else's." In essence, the honor defense equates a wife's adulterous act (or allegedly adulterous act) with a physical act of aggression by the accused. As one criminal defense lawyer told Americas Watch, "if the law foresees the legitimate defense of physical integrity it can also understand that the man has rights to defend his interior life, though the law does not foresee this....Nonetheless, if someone takes away your motive to live [honor], its worth more than life."[44] As with legitimate self-defense, a successful honor defense results in acquittal.

The notion that a man's honor can be gravely threatened by his wife's adulterous action reflects proprietary attitudes towards women deeply rooted in Brazilian society. When Brazil's first Civil Code was passed in 1914, women were considered perpetual wards, like minors and the elderly. Although by 1932 a woman could vote and by 1962 she could work outside the home without her husband's permission, she still had subordinate status as he was deemed head of the household and was the one "authorized to represent the family legally, to administer the family's

---

[42] Corrêa, *Os Crimes Da Paixão*, p. 22.

[43] Brazilian Penal Code, Article 28.

[44] Attorney Clóvis Sahione, interview with Americas Watch, April 1991.

finances, and to support the family."[45] The 1988 Constitution grants full equality to women but the Civil Code has yet to be changed.

This subordinate status is the basis for the belief that the wife is the husband's property and any action by her which does not fall within the prescribed conjugal norm, especially adultery, constitutes an offense against his honor. Brazilian family law experts writing in the 1950s described it this way:

> When a man violates the conjugal loyalty he does that by futile desire. That doesn't destroy the love of the woman, or the fundament of conjugal society. The woman's adultery, on the contrary, affects the family's internal order, compromising the stability of the conjugal life. The woman's adultery is more serious, not only for the scandal it causes, but also because it hurts the moral values and the law more deeply. There is the danger of her introducing strange children to her home."[46]

In many cases, a successful honor defense depends less on showing the accused's passion or lack of intent to kill than on demonstrating the husband's honor and the wife's dishonorable behavior within a recognized conjugal relationship.[47] For example, in one 1957 case of attempted murder, the husband suspected that his wife was having extra-marital affairs. He found her sitting on the couch at home with an electrician whom he believed was her lover, became enraged and shot them both. He later told his mother who was elsewhere in the house that he had "cleansed his honor." The electrician later testified that he had been

---

[45] de Fonseca, Dr. Romy Medeiros, op. cit., p. 16.

[46] Lopes de Oliveira, Manual de Direito da Família (Manual of Family Law) 1986, cited in Corrêa, *Morte Em Família*, p. 89.

[47] As noted in *Quando A Vítima É Mulher*, a study prepared for the National Council on the Rights of Women, the jury "doesn't evaluate the crime in itself, but instead evaluates the victim and the accused's life, trying to show how adapted each one is to what they imagine should be the correct behavior for a husband and wife....The man can always be acquitted if the defense manages to convince the jury that he was a good and honest worker, a dedicated father and husband, while the woman was unfaithful and did not fulfill her responsibilities as a housewife and mother....This way the ones involved in the crime are judged distinctly. Men and women are attributed different roles, in a pattern that excludes citizenship and equality of rights."

called to the house by the husband. The defendant was acquitted on legitimate defense of honor.[48]

In a 1970 case a woman decided to leave her husband after 17 years of marriage. The husband suspected she was leaving him for another man, locked her in the bedroom, and killed her. In court proceedings he was described as a good worker and a good father. She was portrayed as a "vain slut" who liked clothes and had many different pairs of shoes. The lover was never found and never testified. The husband was acquitted on legitimate defense of his offended honor.[49]

In a third case in 1972, the couple had been married for 16 years. All was well in the marriage until she got a job, began coming home late and, according to testimony from the accused, refused to pay her "conjugal debt." He killed her and was acquitted, again on legitimate defense of honor. The decision was upheld on appeal.[50]

One São Paulo Supreme Court judge acting in a 1958 case acquitted a husband of a double homicide of his wife and her lover. He explained it this way:

> Our customs, may God preserve them, and our legislators' spirits allow us to recognize legitimate defense of honor when a wife is caught in the act (of adultery). To judge otherwise is to go against our moral values and the purity of our customs. To deny legitimate defense of honor means to make it impossible for an unfortunate husband whom fate caused to suffer great pain to defend himself, since this is his only argument.[51]

As these cases demonstrate, the honor defense has been successfully invoked in Brazil as if it were the equivalent of legitimate self-defense, with the defendant's resulting acquittal. Yet at no point does the law equate a threat to a man's honor with the danger posed by an imminent physical attack. The legitimate defense of honor accepts not only that a wife's adultery constitutes such an "imminent threat," but also, as in the cases described above, that her merely alleged adultery or desire to

---

[48] Corrêa, Mariza, *Morte Em Família*, Graal (Rio de Janeiro, 1983) p. 132.

[49] Ibid., p. 113.

[50] Ibid., p. 126.

[51] Unnamed judge cited in Correa, *Os Crimes de Paixão*, p. 66.

separate or refusal to engage in sexual relations constitute such a threat as well.

Moreover, the notion that the accused reacted to a "present or imminent threat" presumes the absence of premeditation by the accused. Yet, the courts have repeatedly upheld the honor defense in cases, like the electrician's case mentioned above, which contain strong evidence of a planned murder.

In addition, a key aspect of the self-defense rule is proportionality of the means employed. The accused must "use the necessary means in moderation" in responding to an imminent threat. Even assuming that a wife's act of adultery tarnished her husband's honor, homicide, or in some cases double homicide, is obviously not a proportionate response. Yet, the Brazilian courts have repeatedly legitimated such disproportionate responses.

The Honor Defense Today

For the past fifty years, Brazilian women have been caught in the middle of a dangerous ambiguity in Brazilian jurisprudence regarding the legitimate defense of honor. At the root of this ambiguity is a tension between the rule of law and the influence of prevailing social norms. On the one hand, the honor defense has absolutely no basis in law and should be rejected. On the other hand, social norms allow that a man can legitimately kill his allegedly adulterous wife on the grounds of honor, and this attitude has acquired the force of law through repeated judicial sanction.

As early as 1955, Brazil's high court began to overturn cases involving acquittal on the grounds of honor. In one 1968 decision, the court found that the "legitimate defense of honor does not exist in a homicide committed by a husband during a crisis of indignation, when the wife has threatened the conjugal honor."[52] Although by Brazilian law the high court's decisions refer only to the specific case being judged and have no precedential value, its decisions in practice carry significant jurisprudential weight and are expected to establish precedent, particularly at the appellate court level. In honor defense cases, however, the high court's decisions have had no such unifying effect and, consequently, a history of contradictory jurisprudence has evolved.

---

[52] Records of the Superior Tribunal Federal, the appellate court of last resort prior to the 1988 constitutional amendments creating two high courts of appeal, one for civil and criminal cases and one for constitutional matters.

For example, a review of appellate court records for the state of Rio de Janeiro from 1978 to 1987 reveals this long-standing contradictory trend. Of 20 cases involving the legitimate defense of honor, eight contained outright and principled rejections of the defense. In one 1979 case, the tribunal found that "the Penal Code doesn't allow a man to decree the death penalty to an unfaithful wife or lover." In a 1983 case, the court found that, as quoted above, "recognizing legitimate defense of honor is equivalent to establishing the right to kill, once social prejudices are accepted."

However, another five cases, upheld the honor defense. In one 1984 case involving an attempted murder, the appellate court found:

> [the victim,] who was in matrimonial litigation with the defendant demanded he pay alimony. That should have made her adopt a more strict behavior to justify the onus she wanted to put on her ex-husband. However, she showed up in the company of an ex-employee said to be her lover, and caused a completely legitimate reaction on the part of the defendant under the point of view of the defense of his hurt honor.

In another attempted murder case in 1981, the defendant was acquitted on the grounds that the victim, his wife's lover, was "an audacious disturber of his conjugal peace." In a 1985 case the murderer was acquitted on the grounds of honor due to "unjust provocation of the victim."[53]

The ongoing tension in Brazilian jurisprudence concerning the honor defense most recently expressed itself in conflicting judicial decisions surrounding the case of João Lopes, a bricklayer who stabbed to death his wife and her lover after catching them together in a hotel room in the city of Apucarana. On March 11, 1991, the Superior Tribunal of Justice, Brazil's highest court of appeal in criminal and civil cases, overturned lower and appellate court decisions acquitting Lopes of the double homicide on the grounds of legitimate defense of honor.

The Court nullified the lower courts' decisions on the grounds that they were against all facts in the case. It found that "honor is a personal attribute which is the property of each spouse. There is no offense to the husband's honor by the wife's adultery. There is no such conjugal honor." In addition, the high court found that "homicide is not an

---

[53] Tribunal of Justice of Rio de Janeiro, Division of Jurisprudence, records for 1978 to 1987.

appropriate response to adultery" and "given that there was no proof of revenge on the part of the wife, the adultery does not place the husband in a state of self–defense as contemplated by the Penal Code."[54] Finally, the court proclaimed that what is defended in such cases "is not honor but the pride of the Lord who sees his wife as property."[55]

The high court's decision was welcomed both internationally and in Brazil as signalling the end of the honor defense. The *Jornal do Brasil*, a leading Rio daily, commended the court's decision saying it was "historic. It buries the thesis of legitimate defense of honor."[56]

However, when the *Lopes* case was re–tried on August 29, 1991, the lower court ignored the high court's ruling and again acquitted Lopes of the double homicide on the grounds of honor. Although the high court in *Lopes* rejected the defense as inconsistent with both the law and the facts, the lower–court judge who presided over the second trial ruled that the honor defense was "essentially the heart" of the matter. The judge told reporters that "one decision of the Supreme Court does not necessarily form a national precedent."[57] The lower court's ruling is particularly significant because the second jury's decision is definitive and cannot be appealed again, unless on other grounds.

The Response of the Courts

Several criminal justice officials interviewed by Americas Watch argued that in the absence of precedential authority at the high court level, lower court judges cannot be held accountable for the honor defense's continued success. One criminal court judge told Americas Watch that the real culprits in honor defense cases are the juries. "The popular jury trials for murder leave the prosecutor with no recourse. He can appeal a jury verdict or a sentence and be supported by the higher court, as in *Lopes*, but each case returns to the state jury tribunal...In this

---

[54] The Court's emphasis on the absence of revenge on the wife's part served to negate the possibility that her actions were consciously designed to attack her husband thereby causing him to defend himself.

[55] Decision of the Superior Tribunal of Justice, March 11, 1991.

[56] *Jornal do Brasil*, March 18, 1991.

[57] State Judge Luis Fernando Araujo, quoted in *Associated Press*, September 2, 1991.

jury system the jury decides according to its conscience not according to the law."[58]

Similarly, a prosecutor in Pernambuco told Americas Watch "the jury doesn't want to know about the law. She demeaned him. So to wash his honor, he killed her. The patriarchal concept is very strong." In his view, "the citizens don't judge correctly. In the interior [juries] don't conform to the expectations of society. Justice is limited. A man kills his wife and goes back on the street."[59] He estimates that in the country's interior the honor defense is still successful 80 percent of the time.

The defense attorney in *Lopes* told Americas Watch in April that "it's not the legal system, but macho society that acquits wife-killers....Society talks louder than the courts."[60] He was certain that the high court's decision would have no impact on the jury tribunal and, as it turned out, rightly expected that the honor defense would be upheld by the jury when the case was re-tried in the lower court in August.

The argument that juries, not judges, are responsible for the continued success of the honor defense has some basis in Brazilian law. In all criminal and civil cases, except homicide, the judge is the sole adjudicator. In homicide cases, however, the popular jury assumes the responsibility for deciding cases and the judge has remarkably little control over the legal or factual basis for its verdict. Judges can dismiss cases for lack of evidence[61] or acquit defendants when convinced that there was no intention to commit a crime,[62] but have they limited authority to impede the arguments of either party and almost no authority to exclude evidence.[63] The lower court judge in the *Lopes* decision told reporters that "unless the defense's strategy is completely absurd or irrelevant, I can do nothing to impede it."[64]

---

[58] Judge Paulo Lemos, interview with Americas Watch, May 1991.

[59] State prosecutor Avilar Caribe, interview with Americas Watch, April 1991.

[60] Attorney João Batista Cardoso, interview with Americas Watch, May 1991.

[61] Criminal Procedure Code, Article 409.

[62] Criminal Procedure Code, Article 411.

[63] Any and all evidence presented by counsel is admissible in homicide cases as long as it was not obtained by illicit means and is relevant.

[64] State Judge Luis Fernando Araujo, quoted in *Associated Press*, September 2, 1991.

Several constitutional and criminal attorneys interviewed by Americas Watch stressed the limited authority of trial court judges. Under Article 483 of the Criminal Procedure Code, the judge cannot interfere in the jury's decision in any way and is largely restricted to posing the questions which the jury will answer in deciding the case. The jury's verdict is sovereign, and can only be appealed if it is against all material evidence in the case or if procedural irregularities occurred in the course of the trial or sentencing. The *Lopes* case, for example, having been appealed once on the merits, cannot be appealed again unless procedural irregularities are discovered.

In principle, Americas Watch does not dispute the desirability of the jury's sovereignty. Rather, we are concerned about the propensity of judges in honor defense cases to defer to that sovereignty even when the jury's verdict is not supported by the law or the facts. For example, the Superior Tribunal's decision in *Lopes* was split 3–2 because the minority favored deferring to the jury's sovereignty, despite the lack of legal or factual basis for the honor defense. Similarly, a Rio appellate court in 1978 upheld an honor defense – appealed on the grounds that it was against all material evidence – because "the jury is the expression of the common sense in the place the crime happened. It expresses the ethical sense of the society from which the jurors are drawn."[65]

While the jury is sovereign, its sovereignty does not extend to deciding contrary to law or against all material evidence. The Superior Tribunal in *Lopes* reversed on both grounds. While its decision is not binding, it does constitute an interpretation of the law which should guide lower court decisions in specific cases. The judge presiding at Lopes's second trial should have instructed the jury in the law consistent with the high court's decision. By permitting the jury to acquit Lopes on the grounds of honor a second time, the judge subordinated his role as guardian and explicator of the law to the whim of a jury ignorant of the law and motivated by social prejudice. To ignore a landmark ruling by the nation's highest court in the very same case makes a mockery of the appellate process and the administration of justice in Brazil.

If judges are prevented from instructing juries in the law, then the Criminal Procedure Code should be amended accordingly. Moreover, judges should use the discretion available to them under existing procedure to inform juries that the honor defense does not exist in law and that no person has a legal right to commit murder on the grounds of offended honor. They should use what authority they have to exclude

---

[65] Tribunal of Justice, Rio de Janeiro, court records from 1979 to 1987.

evidence[66] relating to the defense of honor -- it is unacceptable that an invalid legal theory or facts supporting it are deemed "relevant" by the courts.

Judges perhaps more than any other civilian authorities have a responsibility to uphold the law and ensure that it is respected. To the degree that they continue to allow the legitimate defense of honor to be successfully argued in Brazilian courts they abrogate this responsibility and perpetuate a culture of impunity in wife-murder cases which puts every Brazilian woman at risk. Only a consistent rejection of the honor defense at all levels of the criminal justice system will ensure its demise.

C. Privileged Homicide

Violent Emotion

Even when the honor defense is not invoked, Americas Watch found ample evidence that the Brazilian courts treat defendants in wife-murder cases more leniently than others arrested for murder, largely through the misuse of the "violent emotion" exception to mitigate sentence. The Penal Code explicitly states that "emotion or passion does not preclude criminal responsibility," but "violent emotion right after the unjust provocation of the victim"[67] is a mitigating circumstance in cases of homicide or attempted homicide. Such crimes are deemed "privileged homicides" and carry a sentence of 1 - 6 years. By contrast, intentional homicides carry a 12 - 30 year sentence.

For the violent emotion exception to apply, the accused must have acted under the influence of spontaneous emotion resulting from some provocation of the victim. As one judge told Americas Watch

> passion doesn't justify the crime....Crimes of passion are committed in a moment of violent emotion, a moment of extreme passion where reasoning is clouded to the point that he practices something crazy with apparent justification.[68]

---

[66] Criminal Procedure Code, Article 408. The commentary attached to this article points out that while judges have no initiative in the initiation of the process, they have "broad powers to direct the process and investigate the truth (*amplos poderes na direção do processo e na apuração da verdade*).

[67] Penal Code, Article 28.

[68] Judge Roberto Ferreira Lins, interview with Americas Watch, April 1991.

The privilege is based on the theory that the "passional criminal" is not dangerous *per se*--rather, the accused acted in a moment of violent emotion which is unlikely to repeat itself. As one jurist noted, in theory the privileged homicide "is an accident in the life of a good man."[69]

In principle, Americas Watch accepts that the extent to which a crime was premeditated or the result of momentary passion should be weighed in determining the crime's severity. We are concerned, however, that the "violent emotion" exception is often misapplied to benefit defendants in wife-murder cases who have shown substantial premeditation. In addition, it is often accepted with little or no evidence of an "unjust provocation" by the victim. Thus, murderers who should have received a minimum twelve-year sentence sometimes serve as little as 18 months.

In the wife-murder cases investigated by Americas Watch, the courts seemed unusually willing to overlook evidence of intentional homicide on the part of the accused and focus instead on the behavior of the victim and its alleged provocative effect. For example, in the 1989 *Aníbal Maciel de Abreu e Silva* case the court granted the "violent emotion" mitigation despite clear evidence that the crime was both deliberate and premeditated. Moreover, the alleged provocation was never actually proven in court. The following is a summary of the case:

On June 3, 1985, Aníbal Maciel de Abreu e Silva shot and killed his ex-wife Nícia de Abreu e Silva, from whom he had been separated for three months. He shot her four times, once in the back.

Several days after the murder, Aníbal presented himself to the police. In his deposition he said he had waited to see Nícia outside the school where she was studying. He was carrying a gun "as usual." He testified that when she came out of the building they got into an argument and he "lost his senses" and killed her. He said he did not premeditate the crime and did not suspect her of having any lovers.[70]

The prosecution charged Aníbal with qualified homicide, aggravated by surprise (medical records showed that Nícia did not physically anticipate the assault) and by base motive, due to his unwillingness to pay the alimony asked for by Nícia pursuant to their separation. This crime carries a minimum sentence of twelve (12) years.

The defense asked that the aggravating factors regarding motive be dropped and that Aníbal be charged with simple homicide, stressing his good antecedents and lack of a criminal record. In classifying the crime the judge retained only the aggravating factor of surprise.

---

[69] Corrêa, Mariza, *Morte Em Família*, Graal (Rio de Janeiro, 1983).

[70] Aníbal Maciel De Abreu e Silva, statement to the police, June 13, 1985.

In the trial, according to testimony given to Americas Watch by the victim's sister, Aníbal's attorney argued that the murder was a privileged homicide committed in a state of violent emotion provoked by the victim. He contended that Aníbal had committed the crime out of jealousy prompted by the fact that Nícia had had three lovers and a lesbian affair with the family's maid.[71] The prosecution contested this defense, pointing out that the accused himself did not suspect a lover. The lovers were never produced, nor was any evidence regarding the maid. The prosecutor further argued that the crime was premeditated. No witness was produced to verify that Aníbal normally carried a gun.

The jury accepted the "violent emotion" defense. In 1989, Aníbal was convicted of privileged homicide and sentenced to 4-1/2 years. Because he was a first-time offender with good behavior he served 18 months in an "open" prison and is presently at liberty. The state prosecutor in the case told Americas Watch that the jury's decision was against all facts in the case. He is appealing the decision on this ground.[72]

Thus, even though there was ample evidence that Abreu e Silva had planned the crime and no evidence to support the defense's claim of provocation by the victim or that the claimed provocation had immediately preceded the murder, the court sentenced the defendant according to the "violent emotion" exception.

A study of violence against women prepared for the National Council on the Rights of Women (CNDM) documents similar misapplication of the "violent emotion" defense in wife-murder cases. It discusses four wife-murder cases in which "violent emotion" was successfully invoked, even though each contained strong evidence of premeditation. Again, little evidence was produced to support allegations of unjust provocation by the victim and in no case was the victim caught in a compromising act immediately before the murder or attempted murder.

Only one defendant of the four, Lindomar Castilho, received a sentence commensurate with the crime of intentional homicide.[73] In the

---

[71] Cecília Barbosa, interview with Americas Watch, April 1991.

[72] Prosecutor Jorge Vacite, interview with Americas Watch, May 1991.

[73] As noted in the background section of this report, Castilho, a famous Brazilian singer, shot his wife Eliane and her cousin, who Lindomar believed was her lover. Eliane died but her cousin survived. The judge accepted Lindomar's "violent emotion" as a rationale for the crime although the prosecutor argued the crime was cruel and premeditated and, in any case, Eliane's active nightlife or alleged love relationship did not constitute provocation of "a crime of this magnitude." Moreover, the existence of a

remaining three cases, one defendant served less than a year in prison, one was acquitted, and one was sentenced to ten years imprisonment but served less than five.[74] In the latter two cases discussed below, the "violent emotion" defense was coupled with an argument for acquittal on the grounds of temporary insanity.

Violent emotion and temporary insanity have been used interchangeably in Brazil to exculpate husbands accused of murdering their allegedly unfaithful wives. Defense attorneys argue that the "violent emotion" provoked by the victim was so strong that it caused the accused to commit the unlawful act in a moment of temporary insanity. While the violent emotion defense only leads to a reduction of sentence, the temporary insanity defense negates criminal responsibility altogether.

In one 1981 case examined in the CNDM study, Francisco Carlos Neto stabbed to death his wife Marinete from whom he had been separated for two years. Testimony in the case indicated that Francisco had threatened to "finish with Marinete" in the past because she had sought alimony after their separation. The defense sought Francisco's absolution on the grounds that he was not in full possession of his mental faculties at the time of the crime. However, a psychological report ordered by the judge determined that Francisco was criminally responsible and aware of the consequences of his act. Nonetheless, the jury found that he was not mentally responsible and acquitted him.[75]

In the second case, Eduardo Arvid Johnston shot his ex-wife to death. Testimony in the case showed that Eduardo had threatened to kill her several times in the past, that he had traced her to her friend's house "where they usually had feminist meetings," followed her car, cut in front of it at an intersection and in a moment of rage shot her five times. She died instantly. The defense argued that Johnston's violent emotion had amounted to temporary insanity. However, the judge found that Johnston was criminally responsible and ordered his pre-trial detention. The jury ultimately rejected the "violent emotion" defense, but found that Johnston did suffer "perturbation of his mental health." The judge set a base

---

relationship between Eliane and her cousin was never substantiated. Women's rights activists immediately protested the judge's ruling in favor of "violent emotion." In 1984 the jury ultimately rejected the "violent emotion" theory and Lindomar was sentenced to 12 years in prison.

[74] *Quando A Vítima É Mulher* (When the Victim is a Woman), Conselho Nacional Dos Direitos Da Mulher, Brasília (CEDAC, 1987), pp. 65-67.

[75] Ibid., p. 76.

sentence of 15 years, but considered Johnston's "mental perturbation" as a mitigating factor and sentenced him to 10 years. Since Johnston had already been imprisoned for four years pending trial, he was released that same year on grounds of good behavior.

In both cases, despite evidence of premeditation, the defense successfully invoked the temporary insanity defense although in *Johnston* it served only to mitigate sentence. In the *Neto* case in particular, strong evidence that the defendant was criminally responsible was overshadowed by the notion that the victim's behavior had in some way provoked her own murder. The "provocation" in that case consisted of seeking alimony.

Americas Watch investigated an October 1990 wife-murder case which--although not yet concluded--initially fit this same pattern. The victim, 28-year-old neurologist Daisy Carreiro, had just decided to separate from her husband, Dr. Ricardo Simonetti, after several beatings. She had gone to live with her mother. On October 12, Simonetti called Daisy's mother's house and asked to see his daughter Rebecca. Daisy dropped Rebecca off with him and agreed to pick her up the next day. When she returned at the agreed upon time, Rebecca was not there and Simonetti killed her with three pistol shots.

Later that day Simonetti was picked up by police and questioned. By his own admission, contained in two sets of letters he wrote prior to committing the crime, he was disturbed by Daisy's independence and "felt betrayed." He decided to "cleanse my honor with my own hands."

Simonetti's attorney argued that he was not in possession of his mental faculties at the time of the crime and, after questioning by the police, Simonetti was taken to a private mental hospital rather than a prison. The prosecutor, citing the letters written by Simonetti prior to the crime and evidence that he had lured Daisy to the apartment, immediately contested this characterization of the murder. Women's rights activists and colleagues of the victim formed a "Pro-Daisy Committee" to contest allegations that Daisy's unfaithfulness had provoked the crime, and they staged several demonstrations urging the authorities to punish Simonetti.[76]

After several mental examinations ordered by the judge, Simonetti was transferred from the private mental hospital to the prison mental ward, and ultimately to prison. He was charged with homicide committed for a base motive (revenge because she wanted to separate), under dissimulation (he enticed her to the apartment planning to kill her) and

---

[76] Sam Dillon, *Miami Herald*, October 30, 1990.

in a manner which made it impossible for the victim to defend herself. He is currently in prison awaiting trial.

Although these actions do not guarantee that the temporary insanity defense will not be successfully invoked at Simonetti's trial, they do illustrate the capacity of the Brazilian judicial system to apply the law strictly in wife-murder cases and to resist the misapplication of the "violent emotion" defense, especially in cases that have attracted domestic and international attention. However, the on-going need for such attention illustrates that women continue to face the risk of discriminatory treatment in Brazilian courts in wife-murder cases.

A criminal court judge who frequently presides in wife-murder trials acknowledged to Americas Watch the influence of gender biased social norms in wife-murder cases, although he stated that such prejudices do not influence his own decisions. In speaking of the application of the violent emotion defense, he said "the rule in these cases is established by custom. From a society of Latin origins there always prevailed superiority of man over woman....There exists perhaps in all of us a bit of machismo. This evidently influences how such crimes are viewed....The woman has to fight to present alternative facts to society."[77]

Many women's rights advocates feel that without considerable public attention Brazilian courts will remain extremely resistant to such "alternative facts." They have witnessed so many wrongful applications of the violent-emotion defense in wife-murder cases that they have come to view it, like the honor defense, as inherently discriminatory against women. Vilma Lessa, an activist in the northeastern state of Pernambuco whose group Vive Mulher! monitors the government's response to wife-murder crimes, told Americas Watch:

> We don't accept the passion thesis in wife-murder crimes. It's based on social and cultural norms that treat women like cattle. Not just laws, but norms....A woman exists only insofar as she is in relation to a man....So-called passion arises the moment the woman breaks the rules of the game by having, for example, an extra-marital affair....Norms have changed, but whenever a woman is murdered, it's as if there has been no advance in these norms. She disrespected his morals, so he went to violent emotion. People forget that we should be in the realm of facts not morals. But the judge has an understanding

---

[77] Judge Roberto Ferreira Lins, interview with Americas Watch, April 1991.

> of the law that is directed to the questioning of morality and the woman is always transformed into the criminal.[78]

Lessa and her colleague Lúcia Barbosa, whose sister was murdered by her husband, regularly monitor wife-murder cases and help draw attention to discriminatory practices by Brazilian authorities. They told Americas Watch that confronting discriminatory attitudes in the Brazilian criminal justice system is an "uphill battle" which requires constant vigilance and involves considerable personal risk. Lessa told Americas Watch:

> If I as an outspoken feminist were murdered here, my assailant would probably be acquitted. I am outside the norms, in a law that is macho, outdated, bitter, old and rancorous. I would not be perceived as an honest women....If I were killed here, which is a possibility, only the women's movement would keep me protected."[79]

According to several prosecutors and judges with whom Americas Watch spoke, the "violent emotion" defense is rarely used in cases in which wives kill their husbands. One state prosecutor told us that "in general, women who kill their husbands are always sentenced to a higher sentence than men who kill their wives....Most men who are accused of killing their wives get simple homicide. Many of the women accused of killing their husbands get qualified homicide."[80]

One judge told Americas Watch that the difference in sentencing between men and women "is related to the fact that men kill their wives in the heat of the moment while women in the great majority plan. Men normally act in an impetuous moment, although it is important to stress that they also plan."[81]

---

[78] Vilma Lessa, interview with Americas Watch, April 1991.

[79] Ibid.

[80] State prosecutor Avelar Caribe, interview with Americas Watch, April 1991.

[81] Judge Roberto Ferreira Lins, interview with Americas Watch, April 1991. Judge Lins noted that women often plan to murder their husbands because it would be fatal to them if they did not. He pointed out that many of the husband-murder cases he has judged involved a long history of battery prior to the homicide. In the United States, in some states prior incidents of battery can be cited as evidence that the accused, even if

The implications of such discriminatory treatment are devastating. When wife–murder cases reach the courts there is considerable risk that female victims will not receive equal protection and that their murderers––if only because of undue reduction of sentence––will receive the implicit sanction of the judiciary.

Despite this disturbing history of misapplication of the violent emotion defense, Americas Watch does not advocate its elimination, since we have understood that there are valid reasons for its application in certain cases. Rather, we urge narrowly defined judicial standards to ensure that it is applied only in appropriate circumstances and in a non–discriminatory manner consistent with equal protection requirements of international law.

Reduced Charges in Wife–Murder Cases

Americas Watch is also concerned about the tendency of the Brazilian criminal justice system to reduce the severity of the charges in wife–murder cases. Although documentation is limited, several women's rights activists and attorneys with whom Americas Watch spoke described a consistent pattern of police, prosecutors and judges reducing charges in such cases with a corresponding reduction of penalty.

Under Brazilian law, the prosecutor has the responsibility of bringing charges against the accused based in part on the police investigation. At any time before forwarding the case to the judge, the prosecutor on his own can reduce the charge if he finds persuasive grounds to do so. To bring a more serious charge, the prosecutor must re–open the case for new evidence from the defense. In either case, the judge then reviews the evidence and affirms or alters the charge.

In the wife–murder cases investigated by Americas Watch, we found several instances in which charges were reduced, often with dramatic effect on punishment.

In one case examined in a 1983 study of death in the family, the accused and his wife lived in a different state than the one where the murder occurred. They had regularly traveled together to another state for his medical treatment. The husband was upset at his wife because she wanted to return home instead of staying with him during his treatment. He said he shot her in a moment of passion because she wanted to return home to have an affair. The wife, who survived the shooting, said her

---

she killed her husband when he was asleep, for example, was acting in legitimate self–defense. Americas Watch is unaware of any husband–murder cases in Brazil which have been successfully argued along these lines.

husband had told her not to wear a cosmetic. When she wore it anyway, he shot her.

The prosecutor charged the accused with aggravated attempted homicide, which carries a minimum prison sentence of 12 years. However, the judge reduced the charge to simple homicide, which carries a minimum prison sentence of six years, noting that the woman was of "bad behavior. Even though married, and a mother of four, she led a futile life and used scandalous clothes, provoking other men's desires. She did that despite her husband's poor health." He later reduced charges further to "grave corporal lesion," which meant that it no longer required a jury trial and rested solely on the judge's adjudication. The accused was sentenced to two years in prison. The defense appealed the sentence on the grounds that the crime was committed under the influence of "violent emotion," and the trial judge reduced the prison term to one year.[82]

A more recent case investigated by Americas Watch also involved a reduction of the charge, although in this case the official responsible was the prosecutor rather than the judge. The victim, Maria Celsa Conceição, got into a fight with her lover, Domingos Sávio from whom she was attempting to separate for the fourth time. According to Celsa's statement to Americas Watch, Sávio went to her apartment where, during the course of an argument, he threw alcohol over her and held her over a lit stove burner. Celsa lost part of her ear and part of her mouth and was badly burned over most of her body. She was pregnant at the time and had to undergo an abortion due to the medications required for the burns. Sávio alleged that Celsa had immolated herself.[83]

The prosecutor filed charges under Section 129 of the Penal Code: causing "grave corporal lesion," aggravated by the permanent deformity of the victim and by the abortion she underwent as a result of the crime. However, according to Maria Celsa's statement to Americas Watch the police chief with whom she spoke and who initiated the investigation of the crime said she had "every means to claim this was an attempted homicide,"[84] which carries a much higher penalty and requires a jury trial. According to representatives of Brazil's National Council of Women (CNDM), cases like *Sávio* "signify an error of classification:

---

[82] Corrêa, Mariza, Morte em Família, Graal (Rio de Janeiro, 1983), p. 140.

[83] Maria Celsa Conceição, interview with Americas Watch, April 1991.

[84] Ibid.

crimes of corporal lesion instead of attempted homicide downgrades the real seriousness of the crime...."[85]

Ultimately, Sávio was acquitted of the crime, largely because the prosecutor felt Maria Celsa was not a credible witness. The prosecutor told the judge that Celsa was "of bad moral behavior because she had a lover when she was dating the defendant" and that "the victim's bad background gives little credibility to her words...."[86] In the absence of any alternative assessment, which traditionally would have been provided by the prosecution, the judge acquitted Sávio. Celsa was in the hospital when the judgment occurred and by the time she learned of it the time in which to file an appeal had lapsed.

A third case investigated by Americas Watch -- which has yet to be tried -- also reflects a controversial classification of the crime by the prosecution. José Fernando Gomes, a 51-year-old dentist, killed his ex-sister-in-law and shot and severely wounded his ex-wife and his sister. His ex-wife is now paralysed and can only move her eyes and lips. Gomes was seen at the scene of the crime and later told the police that he suspected his ex-wife was having an affair with another dentist.[87]

Both the police and prosecution charged one count of homicide and two counts of grave corporal lesions. An attorney hired to represent Gomes' ex-wife Katia argued that one homicide and two attempted homicides should have been charged.[88]

In only one case investigated by Americas Watch was the victim, who was represented by a private lawyer, able to sustain the original charge of aggravated attempted homicide. In this case, which resembles that of Maria Celsa Conseição described above, Christina Lopez Afonso and her lover had agreed to separate when she decided to live abroad. According to testimony given to Americas Watch by the victim, her lover then changed his mind about the separation. He came to her house, got drunk and began throwing things around the apartment. He then threw alcohol on her and lit her on fire with a match. She was burned over 65 percent

---

[85] National Council for the Rights of Women, press release, undated.

[86] Promotor José do Espirito Santo Domingues Ribeiro, final arguments to the judge, Porto Velho, June 12, 1991.

[87] José Fernando Gomes, statement to the police, Recife, Pernambuco, February 15, 1991.

[88] Criminal lawyer Bráulia Lacerda Braulio, interview with Americas Watch, April 1991.

of her body. Her lover was charged and found guilty of "attempted homicide aggravated by cruel means."

Christina, who now works in a center for burn victims, told Americas Watch that in her view the reason her lover was convicted was that the judge "refused to allow questions of morality to enter into the arguments. Neither the defendant's nor my morals were ever examined." She noted that "the old arguments continue to condemn women and free men by transforming the woman into a panther who provoked the crime. My case is having the opposite effect." However, of similar cases with which Christina is familiar, "mine is the only one I know of in which the man went to prison."[89]

In theory, the classification of a crime depends entirely on the intent of the accused. However, the court's assessment of that intent often appears to be clouded by discriminatory attitudes towards the female victim with the result that charges are often reduced unjustifiably.

Again, information in this area is too scarce from which to draw broad conclusions about a pattern of undue leniency. Nonetheless, the cases discussed above are examples of what was repeatedly described to us as a pattern in which the courts systematically charge lesser crimes in wife-murder cases, thereby assuring lower sentences.

Preferential Treatment of Offenders

The lenient treatment accorded assailants in wife-murder cases, as described above, is especially troubling because a large majority of defendants are already "privileged" under Brazilian law as first-time offenders.[90] As one defense attorney interviewed by Americas Watch noted, "you don't kill your wife twice."[91] Because such offenders are

---

[89] Christina Lopes Afonso, interview with Americas Watch, May 1991.

[90] Several activists interviewed by Americas Watch pointed out that first-time-offender status would be denied to any perpetrator who had a previous record, and that many wife-murder crimes culminate a long period of domestic abuse. Unfortunately, as detailed in the section of this report on battery, such crimes often are not reported to the police, or, more important, when reported, are not always registered in an official police bulletin. And, even when registered, they are rarely prosecuted. Thus a wife-murderer who is a "first time offender" might actually have a history of committing domestic abuse, but it would not necessarily have been registered with the authorities.

[91] Attorney Clóvis Sahione, interview with Americas Watch, April 1991.

often people of good standing with no prior record, the large majority not only defend their cases while at liberty but also receive reduced penalties.

The principle of first–time offender was introduced in Brazil in a 1977 Penal Code reform which became known as the *Lei Fleury* (after a notorious police chief who was one of its early beneficiaries). The Fleury Law affects all forms of imprisonment for first–time offenders awaiting trial, sentencing or a decision on appeal. It gives judges discretion at any of these stages to grant liberty to first offenders pending a judicial decision on the merits, so long as there is no cause for preventive detention. Preventive detention is only used by judges to preserve the public order and to ensure the appearance of the accused at trial or pending appeal. The 1990 heinous–crimes law modified the Fleury Law, exempting from its benefit first–time offenders accused of heinous crimes, including rape.

While Americas Watch fully endorses the concept of reasonable bail for criminal defendants, it is concerned that social prejudices lead judges to release offenders in wife–murder cases far more often than in other homicide cases, even when there is a legal basis for their detention. According to several defense attorneys and judges interviewed by Americas Watch, an estimated 90 percent of the defendants who are convicted in wife–murder cases pursue their case without ever spending a night in prison until they are finally sentenced, which is often years later.

In the *Aníbal Abreu e Silva* case discussed above, the prosecution requested the preventive detention of the accused on the grounds that he had fled the scene of the crime and retained ample means to flee the country. The judge denied the prosecution's request, leaving Anibal to pursue his case in liberty, a status which benefits the accused in several ways, which includes exacerbating the judicial system's already chronic delay. As one defense lawyer noted, "time gained by being at liberty works in favor of the accused. Society begins to forget."[92] Moreover, according to judges and prosecutors with whom we spoke, offenders in wife–murder cases often take advantage of their freedom to flee, thereby rendering prosecution––which in Brazil requires the presence of the accused––practically impossible.

In the *Gomes* case discussed above, the judge granted a controversial petition for habeas corpus prior to the accused's arrest on the grounds that he was a first–time offender with a good background. The court hearing on habeas corpus was postponed several times and Gomes remained at

---

[92] Zulaiê Ribeiro, interview with Americas Watch, April 1991.

liberty, even though another judge had issued an order for his preventive detention on the grounds that he was "dangerous and represents a criminal threat to society." On August 1, 1991, the state court granted the habeas corpus petition annulling the preventive detention order and securing liberty for Gomes for the duration of the trial.

First–offender benefits are also invoked after conviction. One criminal court judge told Americas Watch:

> Our law is loose and sloppy. Somebody's condemned to six years for killing his wife and he's a first–time offender with a good background, he won't even serve 18 months. He usually goes to a semi–open prison and then one year later is granted conditional liberty (*liberdade condicional*) which is not linked to anything. We don't even watch him.[93]

The benefits of provisional liberty for deserving candidates should be preserved, but judges should weigh such liberty against the gravity of the crime, the desirability of speedy justice, and the potential for injustice resulting from flight -- and should not allow social prejudice about the crime to influence their judgment.

******

Americas Watch does not suggest that the Brazilian government is *per se* responsible for deeply rooted social prejudices which underlie the honor defense, misapplication of the violent emotion defense, unwarranted reduction of charges in wife–murders and preferential treatment of offenders. Nor are such discriminatory attitudes unique to Brazil. However, insofar as Brazil's police and judges legitimate such prejudices by routinely allowing them to influence their disposition of wife–murder cases, the government is responsible for failing to fulfill its obligations under both domestic and international law to guarantee equal protection to its citizens without regard to sex.

---

[93] Judge Roberto Ferreira Lins, interview with Americas Watch, April 1991.

IV. BATTERY

A. The Legal Context

Under the Brazilian Penal Code, physical abuse falls into the category of causing corporal lesions (*lesão corporal*), defined in Article 129 as an offense "to someone's physical integrity or health." Such crimes carry a sentence of 3 months to a year.

The Penal Code distinguishes between minor and serious lesions, with the seriousness determining the length of the sentence. Any report of physical abuse must be followed by a visit to the Medical-Legal Institute, or IML, which determines the seriousness of the lesions according to, among other things, the victim's capacity to work, the likelihood of permanent disability, and the existence of major bodily injury which results in loss of function or permanent deformity. Serious abuse can result in a prison sentence of from 1 to 8 years. Beating which ends unintentionally in death carries a 4 to 12 year prison sentence.

As with homicide, penalties are reduced in corporal-lesion cases when the crime is committed unintentionally or immediately after an unjust provocation of the victim. Prison sentences can be replaced by fines when the nature of the offense is not serious.

Crimes of physical abuse are not tried by juries. They are decided by judges pursuant to police reports and the investigations of the prosecution, defense and judge. The manner of prosecuting these cases depends on whether they are classified as public or private action crimes. Crimes which cause serious injury are public action crimes which depend on state initiative for their prosecution. By contrast, private action crimes, which include light lesions and most sexual crimes (see following section), depend on the initiative of the victim, who must file suit. Once suit is filed the victim may at any time discontinue the prosecution. Exceptions to this rule relate to sexual crimes involving serious physical injury, when once the victim initiates the prosecution only the state can stop it.

A woman seeking to report a physical or sexual abuse to the police follows a standard procedure. After reporting to the police station, the complaint is registered in a Bulletin of Occurence by a detective and the woman proceeds to the Medical-Legal Institute (IML) for an examination. After receiving the IML's report the police investigation begins and is overseen by a detective inspector. The results of the inquiry are forwarded to the police chief for review and summation and then passed on to the justice system for prosecution. Though the system works in theory and provides for adequate oversight, Americas Watch found evidence of reports to the police which were never officially registered, registered complaints which were never fully investigated and investigated cases which were never prosecuted.

In addition to criminal penalties, the law provides such remedies for domestic abuse as separation orders and divorce. However, of primary concern for this report is the application of criminal law to physical abuse of women in the home. In general, Americas Watch found that while the creation of women's police stations has greatly enhanced the public visibility of crimes of domestic violence, the formal criminalization of such abuse is the exception rather than the rule.

B. The Response of the Police and the Courts

Prior to the creation of the women's police stations in 1985, police stations rarely investigated crimes of violence against women which occurred in the home. In many cases, police officers were actively hostile towards female victims seeking to report such abuse.

The national anti-violence network SOS-Mulher, which was created in 1981 and aided over 2,000 victims of domestic violence in its first year, found that "violence against women continued in the regular *delegacias* when they tried to report aggressions." The SOS network reported:

> Battery, rape and death threats are routine facts in the lives of many women....Every time women go to the regular *delegacias* looking for support and protection, they suffer another type of violence. This is the violence of refusing to register their complaints, the suspicion cast upon them making them responsible for the crimes they suffered....Such behavior of the authorities reinforces and legitimizes impunity for violence against women and makes them hesitate to fight for their rights.[94]

A 1983 follow-up study in Minas Gerais by the Center for the Defense of Women's Rights found that the police often turned female victims away, on the grounds that domestic violence was "a private problem." When police did register domestic abuse crimes, they frequently failed to follow standard procedures, leaving out pertinent

---

[94] Letter sent to the Secretary of Public Security by the SOS Mulher Chapter in Belo Horizonte, October, 1982, cited in *Crimes Contra A Mulher: A Violêcia Denunciada*, provisional title, unpublished report written by Maria da Conceição Marques Rubinger, et al, with support from the Ford Foundation, 1991.

information about the circumstances of the abuse. In addition, they often subjected the victim to abusive treatment aimed at implicating her in the crime.[95]

An Assistant Secretary of Public Security who served as Secretary of Public Security in Pernambuco prior to and during the creation of the women's *delegacias*, told Americas Watch that "the *delegacia* was created because of the failure of regular police to investigate crimes....The woman was seen as something her husband can beat on. She could be a victim of violence and then have it be perceived by the police as normal. There's a song that says you don't beat a woman even with a flower, but the reality is different."[96]

In the context of such overtly discriminatory attitudes on the part of police, the creation of women's police stations to deal exclusively with violence against women constituted a major victory for women's rights advocates. As noted by Sonia Alvarez, "the ground-breaking recognition of this gender-specific aspect of crime by the State [was] unprecedented in Brazil and indeed the women's precinct structure is unparalleled anywhere in the world."[97]

Brazil's most recent census (1988), coupled with reports gathered from the women's *delegacias*, reveal a high level of domestic abuse among reported crimes of physical violence against women. A 1987 study of over 2,000 battery cases registered at the São Paulo *delegacia* from August to December 1985, found that over 70 percent of all reported crimes of violence against women occurred in the home. Almost 40 percent of these registered incidents involved serious bodily injury, usually committed by the accused's own feet or fists.[98] The 1988 census generally corroborates these figures. These statistics give the first in-depth picture of domestic violence in Brazil.

In the six years since their creation the *delegacias* have succeeded not only in expanding the definition of criminal activity in Brazil to include violence against women, but also in altering the traditional perception of

---

[95] *Crimes Contra A Mulher*, introduction.

[96] Assistant Secretary of Public Security Marini de Figueired, Recife, interview with Americas Watch, April 1991.

[97] Alvarez, Sonia E., *Engendering Democracy in Brazil* (New Jersey: Princeton University Press, 1990), p. 218.

[98] Fundação SEADE, Conselho Estadual Da Condição Feminina, *Um Retrato Da Violência Contra A Mulher*, (CIP International, 1987).

wife–beating as socially acceptable. According to former National Council of Women President Jacqueline Pitanguy:

> The existence of the *delegacias* means that certain acts (which were not and still are not in many cases) perceived as criminal behavior by the regular police, by the accused and frequently by the victim are now qualifying as criminal behaviors. And they are being punished as such. In this sense the *delegacias* not only combat crime but also its definition, changing the border of accepted/non–accepted social behavior.[99]

Despite the *delegacias*' considerable accomplishments in responding to women victims and raising the visibility of domestic violence, Americas Watch found that the actual criminalization of such abuse has not markedly increased. Several researchers told Americas Watch that in general the *delegacias*' impact "has been more psycho–social than criminal. They created a space within the police system which is dedicated to recognizing crimes of violence against women, but have not necessarily worked as an effective deterrent to such violence."

Sociologists, researchers, attorneys and women's rights advocates interviewed by Americas Watch estimated that only 20 to 50 percent of the domestic–abuse cases reported to the *delegacias* are ever investigated. Figures from the main São Paulo *delegacia* show that of 2,573 corporal–lesion cases registered in 1989, only 1,135, or less than 50 percent, were ever investigated by the police.[100]

The reasons for these low investigative rates are complex and vary from police station to police station and state to state. However, general trends are discernible. Most people familiar with the *delegacias* attribute this problem less to the failings of the *delegacias* themselves (although they are a contributing factor) than to the limitations imposed on the *delegacias* by the institutional and social context within which they operate. Many people we interviewed, including *delegadas* (women police officers), attribute low investigation rates primarily to shifting and often diminishing economic and political support from the state and federal governments, low police morale, and lack of training about domestic violence at the police academy.

---

[99] Pitanguy, Jacqueline, "Violence Against Women, Addressing a Global Problem," p. 5.

[100] Assessoria Especial Das Delegacias De Defesa Da Mulher Do Estado De São Paulo, General Statistics, 1989.

The effectiveness of the *delegacias* depends on the importance local authorities ascribe to them. There are only 74 *delegacias* in all of Brazil's 24 states and two territories and they are not equally distributed throughout the country (over 50 are located in the state of São Paulo). Nor do they receive equal support vis-a-vis each other or the regular police stations. Pitanguy notes that "the prestige of the women's police stations inside police structures varies, but in general they are not given the importance of traditional specialized police stations like those for homicide or drugs."[101]

In the state of Rio de Janeiro, for example, the first women's police station opened in 1986 and was soon followed by two more. After a change in government, however, only one *delegacia* was added during the next four years. In the same period, the state of São Paulo added nineteen stations. This may be due partly to economic factors, as Rio suffered a severe economic crisis in the late 1980s. However, the number of *delegacias* is also a function of political will. The new Rio state government – elected in 1990 – has already added two additional women's *delegacias* and plans to add five more by the end of 1991. Rio Secretary of Public Security Nilo Batista told Americas Watch that "the demand is very great."[102]

Several *delegadas* we interviewed spoke of the discriminatory treatment they experience from many of their police colleagues as a result of choosing to work in the women's police stations. One *delegada* told us that the *delegacias* are treated like "the kitchen of the police." A women's rights activist who works closely with the *delegacias* told Americas Watch "the *delegacias* are not a career police thing. There is a stigma attached to working in a *delegacia*. The *delegadas* do not like the work because of discrimination in the police force."[103]

While diminishing resources and poor morale are key factors in low investigative rates by the police, the most regularly cited problem is that many women police serve in the *delegacias* without receiving adequate specialized training. Sonia Alvarez points out that although "in some cases feminist scholars and activists were brought in to train female police at these specialized precincts, feminists were marginalised from

---

[101] Pitanguy, Jacqueline, "Violence Against Women, Addressing a Global Problem," unpublished paper prepared for the Ford Foundation, New York, 1991, p. 6.

[102] Secretary of Public Security Nilo Batista, interview with Americas Watch, April 1991.

[103] Cida Medrado, interview with Americas Watch, April 1991.

most, as the selection and training of staff was entrusted to the local force."[104] In São Paulo and Rio for example, early attempts to have material on domestic violence incorporated into the police training manuals, while successful at first, suffered from both lack of institutional support and financial cutbacks, and were ultimately dropped.

In some *delegacias*, particularly in the early years, lack of police training was offset by the presence of social workers who were trained to respond in domestic violence cases. However, financial cutbacks and lack of internal support have scaled down the capacity of the *delegacias* to provide psychological aid as originally intended. Some cities and states, like São Paulo and the small city of Santo Andre outside of São Paulo, continue to retain social workers in the *delegacias* to assist victims. In the states of Belo Horizonte and Rio de Janeiro, however, *delegacias* no longer provide this service. Overall, the psychological aid provided at the *delegacias* is minimal.

These institutional constraints limit the capacity of the *delegacias* to move beyond raising the visibility of domestic violence to increasing the actual criminalization of such abuse. Attorneys with whom we spoke believe that, in particular, the *delegadas*' lack of training perpetuates a reluctance by police authorities, regardless of their gender, to see domestic violence as a crime. According to Pitanguy "police women still need to perceive certain violent behavior as crimes."[105] As one attorney who frequently represents domestic violence victims in civil cases told Americas Watch, "the *delegacias* normally don't register the crime....There doesn't exist any mentality in the *delegacia* that a crime has occurred....Even the *delegacias* don't consider domestic violence a crime. Even registered cases don't go forward; they get shelved. It's a question of mentality. It's family, it's not a crime."[106]

Even when domestic abuse is perceived as a crime, these attitudes can carry over into the police's choice of the crime to be charged. There appears to be a tendency to file reduced charges in cases of domestic abuse. In the 1987 São Paulo study cited above, for example, researchers noted that in 30 percent of the cases classified as "serious threats" and 36 percent of those classified as "misunderstandings," the

---

[104] Alvarez, p. 246.

[105] Jacqueline Pitanguy, interview with Americas Watch, April 1991.

[106] Cecília Texeira Soares, Pró–Mulher, interview with Americas Watch, April 1991.

police record included complaints of physical abuse which apparently had not been reflected in the crime charged.[107]

These reduced charges are to some extent attributable to lack of training. Detectives, who are often the first to interview the victim, are not always versed in the law pertaining to the classification of domestic-abuse offenses. Although women police chiefs are required to have legal degrees and should correct improper classifications before they are forwarded for prosecution, this is not always the case.

Available data indicates that reduced charges are also due to the police's reluctance to investigate reports of domestic abuse. Researchers at the University of São Paulo Center for the Study of Violence found that "the women police showed a lot of disrespect for the victims. They were not sympathetic, sort of fed-up. They ended up blaming the victims for their own fate."[108] One researcher noted that certain "informal mechanisms" exist to file lesser charges in cases of domestic abuse so that they can be registered as private-action crimes which depend on the initiative of the victim, not the state, for prosecution.

This reluctance to investigate is often due to the *delegadas*' assessment that domestic abuse will not be prosecuted. As one scholar noted, "the *delegadas* are in a double bind. They want to help the victim but they do not want to mislead her about the likelihood that her assailant will be punished."[109] One victim of domestic violence interviewed by Americas Watch had just come from a *delegacia* where the *delegada* told her "it would not do any good to register the crime because 70 percent of such cases are dropped."[110]

Brazil's first chief of a women's police station, Rosemary Correa, now a deputy in the São Paulo State Legislature, estimates that 40 percent of domestic abuse cases are prosecuted. However, the main *delegada* in Rio told Americas Watch that of the over 2,000 battery cases she investigated in 1990, none resulted in punishment of the accused. Similarly, the U.S. State Department's human rights report for 1990 noted that in the main *delegacia* in São Luis, Maranhão, of over 4,000 complaints registered by

---

[107] *Um Retrato Da Violência Contra A Mulher*, p. 44.

[108] Nancy Cardia, sociologist, University of São Paulo's Center for the Study of Violence, interview with Americas Watch, April 1991.

[109] Professor Silvia Pimentel, interview with Americas Watch, April 1991.

[110] "Marta", interviewed by Americas Watch at Pró-Mulher, a legal and social assistance office in Rio de Janeiro, April 1991.

women from 1988 to 1990, only 300 were forwarded for processing by the court and only two men were convicted and sent to prison.[111]

Women police officers in several cities told Americas Watch that even when they investigate cases in a timely manner and forward them for prosecution they do not hear from the prosecutor for months and then he or she is usually seeking additional information.[112] One *delegada* said the prosecutors often sent the files back to the police "due to a back-log in the courts. It's sent back [to the *delegacia*] to buy time." One police chief told Americas Watch that in cases where "it takes a long time, the case can kind of go away."[113] According to one criminal court judge "someone commits a crime and it takes an eternity for it to get a response. This is a great discredit to judicial power." The day before Americas Watch's visit he was presiding in the trial of a case which occurred 17 years ago. While he was quick to point out that this kind of delay "is the exception," he noted that "a lot of these trials go on for years. It's really a structural problem."[114]

The failure to prosecute can also be attributed in part to the nature of domestic violence. In the first place, both prosecutors and judges drop cases when they believe the couple will reconcile. Moreover, in the courts as with the police, there is a persistent failure to see domestic battery as a crime. Judges receive no training on domestic violence. A defense lawyer representing domestic violence victims in Rio de Janeiro told Americas Watch that the "judiciary takes a benign view towards violence against women."[115] Professor Silvia Pimentel told Americas Watch, "Domestic violence is not sufficiently followed by the state. We are seeking improvements in the law and its implementation, but it

---

[111] United States Department of State, Country Reports on Human Rights Practices for 1990, February 1991, p. 531.

[112] Under the law, police have 30 days to complete an initial investigation when the suspect is not detained, and the prosection has another 30 days to conduct its own investigation and recommend charges. However, these limits are regularly exceeded, often without the required judicial authorization.

[113] Detective Inspector, Mary May da Silva Porto, interview with Americas Watch, April 1991.

[114] Judge Roberto Ferreira Lins, interview with Americas Watch, April 1991.

[115] Attorney Leila Linhares, interview with Americas Watch, April 1991. Linhares is a criminal defense attorney who works for CEPIA, an organization which monitors, among other things, penal and judicial response to crimes of violence against women.

requires more than a change in legal framework. It requires a whole change of attitude. A man should not be able to beat and/or kill his wife with impunity."[116]

C. The Woman Victim's Perspective

Lack of economic and political support by state and federal governments, discriminatory treatment of and low moral among women police, lack of police training and, above all else, failure to prosecute domestic abuse all contribute to the denial of equal protection to Brazilian woman victims. But this problem is not due to police or judicial failings alone. Many people with whom Americas Watch spoke also mentioned the hesitation of victims to report the abuse and, more important, the victims' fear of not being able to sustain the effects of criminal prosecution on their own lives.

To some extent a woman's decision to seek judicial assistance depends on her understanding of basic legal rights and her confidence, or the confidence of her family or friends, that she will get justice. Anita, a child-care worker in the Santa Marta *favela* in Rio de Janeiro, who has survived domestic violence herself, told Americas Watch that women in Rio's slums live in a culture of violence and perceive domestic abuse as a normal occurrence. She told us of "Dorina," a woman who used to be her neighbor in Santa Marta:

> Dorina died as a result of a head injury. Every day her husband used to beat her head against the wall. He used to throw her down the stairs. People were used to hearing her being beaten. She died of the beating, but nobody went to call the police. It's no use going to the police, nothing ever happens. There was no police investigation into Dorina's death. Her husband went to her funeral with another woman.

In Anita's own case, her husband did not beat her physically, but abused her psychologically. She said he was afraid her relatives would punish him so he did not beat her. It took her a long time, after repeated incidents of psychological abuse and threats of physical and sexual violation, to seek legal help. She told Americas Watch, "First you have to know you have rights. If you don't know you have rights, you can't advocate for them."

---

[116] Professor Pimentel, interview with Americas Watch, April 1991.

Conversely, women who are aware they have rights sometimes seek to report occurrences which are not fully deserving of police attention. They arrive at the *delegacia* without a clear sense of the police's function and with unrealistic expectations. One victim told Americas Watch that she "expected the police to solve all my problems."

Other women go to the *delegacias* as a last resort when they simply "can't take it anymore," or genuinely fear for their lives. As one victim of domestic abuse told Americas Watch, "I went because he was going to kill me." Their desperation, however, does not necessarily mean they want to press charges against their abuser who, more often than not, is their husband. As one social worker told Americas Watch, "she wants the police to protect her, but she doesn't want an official registration."[117]

While a woman's reluctance to report abuse is often due to psychological reasons, lack of faith in the system, or because of ignorance of her rights, it may also be due to economic realities. Many women victims of domestic abuse have one or more children[118] and are economically dependent on their husbands. The 1987 São Paulo study noted above found that almost 50 percent of the women victims of domestic violence were totally dependent on their spouses for financial support.[119] As Anita, the child-care worker in Santa Marta told Americas Watch, women living in extreme poverty view the situation this way: "Its bad with him, but its worse without him."[120]

Even if women are contributing to the household income, it is extremely difficult for them to survive alone, especially with children. According to recent economic figures for Brazil, "women make up 60.7 percent of all workers earning less than one half of a minimum salary – about $50 per month."[121]

Women are further discouraged by the lack of medium-term protection from the state. Civil remedies, such as protection orders or separation agreements, are available but depend on registering the occurrence with the police. Protection orders in particular are difficult to obtain without strong evidence of serious physical abuse and are rarely

---

117 Cida Medrado, interview with Americas Watch, April 1991.

118 *Um Retrato Da Violência Contra A Mulher*, p. 66.

119 Ibid., p. 6.

120 Anita, interview with Americas Watch, April 1991.

121 Karen Lombardi, *Retrato da Mulher Brasileira*, June 1990, mimeo.

enforced. In addition, these remedies require legal assistance which is not always available. Legal aid from the state in criminal cases is particularly rare and, according to a criminal defense lawyer practicing in the state of Pernambuco, of questionable quality.

Other alternatives, such as public shelters (*abrigos*) do not exist. We found that only one public shelter was operating in Brazil, with a capacity for only 6 women and their children, in a country of 75 million women. In addition, this shelter was designed to service exclusively the relatively small city outside São Paulo in which it is located.[122] Without shelter, women victims of serious domestic abuse, even when they do report the crime, have no alternative in most cases but to return to live with their abuser. Even if the investigation proceeds, it often takes months or years. In the meantime, as one *delegada* said, "the woman is going to get it."[123]

[122] The shelter, located in the city of Santo André, outside São Paulo, was opened in November 1990. The development was unprecedented in that the shelter evolved out of close cooperation between state and city authorities who belonged to different political parties. The shelter works closely with the first women's police station in the city, which opened earlier in the year and provides psychological, legal and employment counselling. As noted, no other comparable facilities exist in Brazil, though a São Paulo-based counseling center, Casa Eliane de Grammont, is in the process of opening a small shelter, and state authorities are planning to re-open the state run shelter Convida which had been closed for some time.

[123] Detective Inspector, Mary May da Silva Porto, interview with Americas Watch, April 1991.

V. RAPE--A CRIME AGAINST CUSTOM?

A. The Legal Context

In addition to crimes of physical abuse, the Penal Code includes crimes defined under Title IV as Crimes Against Custom, of which sexual crimes, classified as crimes against sexual liberty, are a sub-category. These crimes include rape and "unusual" sexual acts--including anal or oral sex, seduction, corruption of minors and abduction by fraud or violence for sexual purposes. The severity of these crimes depends on whether they result in serious bodily injury or death. The penalty can also be increased if the crime is committed by two or more persons or the aggressor abuses a position of authority in relation to the victim.

Under Article 213 of the Penal Code, only a woman can be raped. The crime is defined as "constraining a woman to carnal conjunction using violence or serious threat."[124] Rape does not include anal coitus or any sexual act other than vaginal intercourse involving violence or serious threat.[125]

Proof of rape requires a showing of vaginal penetration and serious bodily injury or a serious threat, by which is meant "the threat of causing serious material or moral damage, for example, death, taking away the means of subsistence or revealing previous criminal or dishonorable acts of the victim."[126] Violence is presumed only in cases involving a girl under the age of fourteen, a mentally retarded woman, or a woman who for other reasons is unable to react.

Rape, like all sexual crimes, is classified as a private-action crime. Thus, in the absence of serious physical abuse, prosecution depends on the initiative of the victim. The victim can change her mind at any time and decline to prosecute. According to Linhares, "Rape is considered a private action crime because it happens to a woman in her intimacy. The state doesn't have a right to expose a woman regarding sexual crimes."[127]

---

[124] Penal Code of Brazil, Article 213.

[125] Penal Code of Brazil, Article 214.

[126] Fernandes Antonio Scarance, Marques Oswaldo Henrique Duek, "*Estupro*" (Rape), paper presented at the 7th Preparatory Seminar for the International Symposium on Victimology of the Institute of Brazilian Lawyers, reprinted in "Doutrina," March 1990.

[127] Attorney Leila Linhares, interview with Americas Watch, April 1991.

Before the enactment of Brazil's first post-colonial Penal Code, in 1830, rape was punishable by death. Today, it is defined as a heinous crime[128] and carries a higher penalty than physical abuse. According to several attorneys, police officers and women's rights activists with whom we spoke, convicted rapists are also severely treated by their fellow prisoners. A woman police chief in Belo Horizonte told Americas Watch of one recent incident in which other prisoners shaved the body of a convicted rapist, sodomized and killed him.[129]

However, while rape has always been viewed as a serious crime in Brazil, penalties for rape have in the past varied according to the "honesty" or "dishonesty" of the victim. Brazil's 1830 Penal Code, while it eliminated the death penalty for rapists, introduced an explicit distinction between "honest" and "dishonest" victims. Rape of an "honest woman" carried a prison sentence of 3 – 12 years. But rape of a prostitute carried a sentence of 1 month to 2 years. "Honesty" was never explicitly defined. Brazil's second Penal Code, enacted in 1890, distinguished between "a virgin (or not) but honest woman" and a "dishonest woman," but again did not define the central term. "Dishonesty" is commonly understood to refer to a "public woman" or prostitute.

Brazil's third Penal Code, which remains in force today, contains no explicit distinction regarding the honesty of a rape victim. Most other sexual acts, however, are crimes only if the victim is an "honest" or "virgin" woman. The crime of seduction, for example, is defined as the act of "seduc[ing] a *virgin woman* between 14 and 18 years old to carnal conjunction, taking advantage of her inexperience or justified confidence."[130] Similarly, the crime of sexual possession through fraud is defined as "inducing an *honest woman* through fraudulent means to practice carnal conjunction."[131]

In theory, removing the explicit reference to the honesty of a rape victim established equal protection for all women. However, many people with whom we spoke emphasized that the distinction between honest and dishonest women, which stems from prejudicial social

---

[128] A 1990 legal reform introduced a definition of heinous crimes, including rape, which permits a judge to decree temporary arrest without bail for thirty days.

[129] Delegada Luiza Adey Mendes, interview with Americas Watch, April 1991.

[130] Penal Code of Brazil, Article 217, emphasis added.

[131] Penal Code of Brazil, Article 216, emphasis added.

attitudes towards women, continues to influence the way the crime of rape is treated by the Brazilian criminal justice system.

The definition of rape as a crime against custom, rather than as a crime against an individual, signifies that the victim is society, not the woman. As noted by sociologists Danielle Ardallion and Guita Debert in a study conducted for the National Council on the Rights of Women (CNDM), "Custom is the juridical object protected in the case. The law punishes the rapist, but is inefficient to recognize the woman's right to her own body and to the free employment of her sexuality. On the contrary, what is defended is a certain kind of morality and a concept of good customs."[132] By law, the woman is only the "passive subject" of rape crimes--her individual rights are seen as less important than the social order which her abuse is seen to violate.[133]

Moreover, the subordination of a woman's right to bodily integrity to the higher judicial good of "custom" opens the door to the honesty distinction. If the victim can be shown not to fit the "customary" role in the first place -- if, for example, she is not a virgin or has engaged in sexual relations outside of marriage -- it will be more difficult to prove that the crime of rape actually occurred.

B. The Response of the Police

Prior to the creation of the women *delegacias* in 1985, sexual crimes were handled by the police stations which specialized in crimes against custom. A 1991 report of the Minas Gerais Center for the Defense of Women's Rights concluded that the treatment of sexual abuse victims in the *Delegacias* of Customs was overtly prejudicial to women -- "from mocking to threats to lack of trust in the victim, several responses are common in daily police practice at the *delegacia*." The Center found that

---

[132] Ardaillon, Danielle and Decert, Evita Grin, *Quando A Vitima É Mulher*, Ist edition, publication of the National Council of Women's Rights, December 1987, cited in *Estupro*, p. 275.

[133] Brazilian feminists believe that what is really protected by the classification of rape as a crime against custom is the female's reproductive function. This is why, in their view, the definition of rape is confined to vaginal penetration: what is really violated in a rape in the eyes of the law is not the individual woman, but society's capacity to reproduce itself through her.

Under Brazilian law, rape victims are exempted from the general ban on abortion, though the process of proving rape is often so lengthy that the woman has the child before the exemption for rape can be certified.

such attitudes on the part of the police had the effect of intimidating the victim, discouraging her from filing a report, and transferring to her the responsibility for the crime.[134]

In rape cases in particular, the police officers' built-in prejudice against the female victim made it even less likely, particularly in cases without severe bodily injury, that they would believe her accusation. One police officer was quoted as saying:

> Nobody is able to spread the legs of a woman if they are crossed, unless she's threatened with a weapon or fears for her life. Most cases happen because the woman consents, because she wants it. Then she regrets it and comes to play victim, comes [and] reports. Many women create favorable conditions for the crime.[135]

The report also cites a case in which a woman reported that she was forced to have intercourse with the aggressor under threat, but the absence of a weapon was seen as evidence that no crime had occurred. One police officer told the Center's researchers "There's no punishment. People will think there is a solution, but it's not true."[136]

After the creation of the women's *delegacias*, which for the most part assumed the functions of the *Delegacias* of Customs, the reporting of rape and other sexual crimes increased dramatically. Whereas only 98 rapes were reported to the Belo Horizonte *Delegacia* of Customs in 1983, almost 300 rapes were reported in 1986 to the women's police station which took its place.[137] Women's *delegacias* in other cities also found that the rate of reported rapes continued to increase. Statistics from São Paulo's *delegacias* show that while only 67 rapes were registered in the main *delegacia* in 1985, 841 rapes were reported in 1990.[138]

---

[134] da Conceição Marques Rubinger, Maria, et al., *Crimes Contra A Mulher: A Violência Denunciada*, (provisional title) forthcoming report prepared with funding from the Ford Foundation, 1991.

[135] Ibid., chapter 5.

[136] Interview with unnamed policeman, cited in *Crimes Contra A Mulher*, chapter 3.

[137] *Crimes Contra A Mulher*, tables 4–6.

[138] Assessoria Especial Das Delegacias De Defesa Da Mulher Do Estado De São Paulo, Boletins De Ocorrencias, 1985 - 1990. This increase in reporting is partly attributable to the increase in the overall number of *delegacias* in São Paulo and their wider geographic distribution.

With the creation of the women's *delegacias,* attitudes towards rape victims also began to change. A study of rape prepared for the National Association of Brazilian Attorneys found that "the *delegacias das mulheres* have given a great contribution to a better assistance to the victims of sexual crimes, with good results in the investigation of the crime and its perpetrator."[139] According to the Assistant Secretary of Public Security of Pernambuco, "Treatment is better in the women's *delegacias*. Women victims of rape can go to a police station and find a woman there and she won't be re-victimized by the police. She is therefore uninhibited in her reporting."[140]

Despite the improved visibility of rape as a crime, Americas Watch found that, as with battery, the number of rapes investigated and prosecuted has not significantly increased. For example, available statistics indicate that of the over 800 cases of rape reported to São Paulo *delegacias* from 1985 to 1989, only 155, or less than one-fourth were investigated.

Since rape as a private cause of action depends on the victim to prosecute, low rates of police investigation are partly attributable to women deciding for their own reasons not to pursue the case. However, available data also suggests that women continue to be discouraged by the treatment they receive by the police. Instead of investigating the rape, the police may even take the opposite approach and reduce the charges. A Detective Inspector at the main *delegacia* in Rio told Americas Watch that "without corporal lesions rape is very difficult to prove. So then the woman's complaint is registered as a threat."[141] Reduced charges of this kind, which may largely result from a lack of training, pose a serious obstacle to efforts to criminalize rape. They downgrade the seriousness of the crime, deny its existence and virtually eliminate the possibility that it will ever be prosecuted.

---

139 Fernandes and Marques, p. 274.

140 Assistant Secretary of Public Security Marini de Figueiredo, interview with Americas Watch, April 1991. While numbers registered with the *delegacias* do indicate a substantial increase in reporting, the figures are, from the perspective of the United States, remarkably low. In 1990, for example, the city of São Paulo, with a population of 11 million people, registered just 392 rapes. By contrast, the city of Washington, D.C., with a population of only 600,000 people, registered 304 rapes. This discrepancy indicates the possibility of significant under-reporting of rape in Brazil. Researchers who conducted a 1987 study of over 2,000 cases reported to the *delegacia* for women in São Paulo in 1985 concluded that the "under registration of sexual occurrences is significant."

141 Detective Inspector da Silva Porto, interview with Americas Watch, April 1991.

In addition, a woman's virginity is still important. The Chief of Rio's main *delegacia*, Marly Preston, told Americas Watch, "When the victim is not a virgin it's harder. With a virgin you can discover recent penetration." While virginity may affect the medical evidence, women's rights activists point out that an overemphasis on virginity opens rape cases to the long-standing - if no longer explicit - legal prejudice against "dishonest" victims. If an unmarried woman is not a virgin, her sexual history is likely to be investigated and her allegation doubted. According to research conducted by the Center for Women's Rights, while the women's *delegacias* are an important improvement, "they have not extinguished the practice of investigating the woman's life."[142]

Within 24 hours of a rape the victim, having already filed a complaint with the police, must by law proceed to the Medical-Legal Institute (IML), the state medical facility responsible for classifying all crimes of physical and sexual abuse. Here, the victim undergoes a medical examination, a crucial element of the rape investigation.[143]

However, the CNDM study cited above found that women do not always follow this procedure. The authors discovered that "women's most common reaction immediately after rape is to shower and throw away the clothes she was wearing before going to the *delegacia*. That keeps the IML from proving the occurrence of carnal conjunction."[144] Even if a woman victim of rape goes immediately to the police and then to the IML, the CNDM study found there is no guarantee the treatment she receives will conform to prescribed procedures.

Although the IML is the only facility accredited by the state to make medical determinations about whether a rape occurred,[145] it suffers from

---

[142] *Crimes Contra A Mulher*, chapter 4.

[143] The IML gathers forensic evidence, such as sperm in the vagina, and again examines the degree of physical abuse, signs of resistance and virginity. The doctors record this information on a standard form.

[144] *Quando A Vítima É Mulher*, p. 21.

[145] Determinations by other medical professionals — the victim's personal physician, for example — are not accepted by the state as evidence. Public or private medical facilities which specialize in violence against women, similar to rape trauma centers in U.S. hospitals, are almost non-existent in Brazil. The city of São Paulo recently began a landmark program opening five sexual-abuse clinics, but this is the only such effort known to Americas Watch in all of Brazil.

a severe shortage of female doctors[146] and makes no provision for training its staff in the treatment of sexual abuse. São Paulo health worker Edna Roland told Americas Watch that this lack of training increases both the trauma experienced by the victims and the potential for misclassifications of sexual abuse crimes.[147]

According to Ardaillon and Decert, the authors of the CNDM study, "many times the medicolegal examination fails to report the signs of physical violence, as if the examination were exclusively gynecological and not of the whole body."[148] The study cites a case in which a nine year old girl was violently raped by her cousin. According to the judge in the case, the IML doctors had "through negligence and carelessness" failed to report the signs of physical violence. Only evidence of forced penetration and the presumption of violence for a victim under age 14 led to the accused's conviction and offset the IML's error.

According to Vilma Lessa, a journalist and activist who monitors violence against women:

> Rape victims go to the IML hoping that the report will be honest and correct. She will be examined to be sure she was raped. She may be questioned about her virginity and sexual history. It is enough to discount the charge if the doctor doesn't find any sperm....She leaves, sure that she has registered the rape. She finds out the hard way that going to the IML was not enough.[149]

State Deputy Rosemary Correa told Americas Watch that "the problem is that [the IMLs] are located only in urban centers and there is a shortage of female doctors. It would make it much easier if a woman could simply go to a hospital for an exam. We have been working on this problem for years." In the meantime, available information suggests that even in cases in which the woman follows prescribed procedures and

---

[146] The state of Rio de Janeiro recently passed a law which requires sexual-abuse victims to be seen by female doctors at the IML. *Delegada* Preston, while welcoming this reform, cautioned that the number of female doctors trained in forensic medicine in Rio is very small. There is no guarantee that the victim will be seen by a female doctor.

[147] Edna Roland, interview with Americas Watch, April 1991.

[148] *Quando A Vitima É Mulher*, p. 21.

[149] Vilma Lessa, interview with Americas Watch, April 1991.

the IML finds evidence of a rape, the case will not necessarily be pursued by the police.

Americas Watch investigated one case of serial rape in the state of Pernambuco in which a prominent local businessman, Eduardo Ximenes, allegedly raped over 22 women. Police records show that at least 15 of the alleged victims registered rape complaints with the police. Court documents regarding one of the victims made available to Americas Watch indicated that she had gone to the IML and the medical findings supported her accusation. Yet, according to the victim's attorney, not a single one of the cases was pursued by the police until a victim's relative came forward and denounced both the police and Ximenes.[150]

Ximenes ultimately was detained by the police in April 1991 under the heinous crimes law, but the police chief's failure to secure an arrest warrant in advance of the arrest led to Ximenes' immediate release. Before a warrant could be issued, Ximenes fled the country and is now at large.

C. The Response of the Courts

In the absence of national statistics on rape which could be compared with statistics for other crimes, it is difficult to determine accurately the degree to which rape, when investigated by the police, is prosecuted in Brazil. However, as mentioned previously, of the over 2,000 crimes of violence against women, including rape, reported to the Rio *delegacia* in 1990, none resulted in punishment of the accused. Similarly, of over 4,000 complaints registered in the women's police precinct at São Luis, Maranhão, between 1988 and 1990, only 300 were forwarded to a court, and only two men were convicted and punished.

However, Ardaillon and Debert found that when rape is actually prosecuted, convicted rapists are often severely sentenced by the courts. Their 1985 study of rape cases in six states concluded that "a number of difficulties hamper the complaint and the beginning process of investigating rape, however, rapists receive relatively long sentences as compared to those convicted of crimes against life."[151] They also discovered that the outcome of a case was often determined by stereotypical attitudes towards both the accused and the victim as described below.

---

[150] Attorney Moacir Veloso, interview with Americas Watch, April 1991.

[151] *Quando A Vítima É Mulher*, p. 22.

Prosecutors Fernandes and Marques, in their study of rape and the Brazilian criminal justice system, also conclude that the "protagonists' stereotypes are decisive elements to the results of the process."[152] They found that rape defendants who are convicted are usually the ones who show alcoholism or drug addiction, have a history of domestic abuse, are unemployed or are "trouble makers." By contrast, acquitted defendants are ones with the opposite qualities--they don't drink and are affectionate, good fathers, hard workers and first-time offenders.

Both studies point out that these characterizations run contrary to evidence that rape "can be committed by men who are normal in all other aspects of their behavior" and that many rapists "come from highly educated and respected families." Ardallion and Debert concluded that men who do not fill the "abnormal" category are "protected by the stereotype of conventional wisdom."[153]

By contrast, many women are not protected by the conventional wisdom. To the degree that they are perceived as deviating from "chaste" and "naive," they will be cast by the defense as "lascivious" and "consenting." In the face of such stereotypes women not only have the burden of proving penetration with violence or serious threat; they must also prove that they are "normal."

Physical injury is often key to proving rape. As one women's rights activist put it, "it is almost as if another crime has to occur in order to prove the existence of rape."[154] In the absence of physical injury, judges, like the police, place great weight on the resistance, or lack thereof, of the victim. Attorney Leila Linhares who works frequently with sexual abuse victims, told Americas Watch that "it's very common in rape trials to blame the victim. If she doesn't have marks of violence she's going to have to prove that a rape took place. There is always a question about whether or not and to what degree she tried to resist and whether or not any rape took place."[155]

Judges assess a victim's resistance based on the seriousness of the physical injury or the threat which accompanied an attack. The difficulty of proving the presence of injury or threat is demonstrated by a March 1991 decision by the Brazilian Superior Tribunal, the same court which

---

[152] Fernandes and Marques, p. 272.

[153] *Quando A Vítima É Mulher*, p. 28.

[154] Attorney Rosane Reis, interview with Americas Watch, April 1991.

[155] Attorney Linhares, interview with Americas Watch, April 1991.

recently overturned the honor defense. The high court found that the presence of a gun during a rape does not constitute "real violence" but only "moral threat." The court's decision, by a vote of four to one, invalidated a lower court's conviction of Celso de Souza Ramos, who had been sentenced to 39 years for three armed robberies followed by rapes. The lower court had decided that Ramos had used real violence because the rapes followed armed robberies and the victims were "dominated by fear and unable to resist." The high court overturned this decision, rejecting the argument that the robberies and the presence of a gun constituted "real violence" to the victim. As a result, Ramos's sentence was reduced from 39 to 33 years and 10 months.[156]

As with the police, the victim's virginity and, by extension, her sexual character are a major issue at the trial. Linhares told Americas Watch that "there is both an implicit and explicit question regarding the victim's honesty. If she is not a virgin and no other physical marks or evidence exist then the situation favors the aggressor. Her honesty and past history are inevitably questioned."[157]

Fernandes and Marques found that, contrary to Article 59 of the Brazilian Penal Code which permits judges to consider the victim's behavior only at the time of the crime, judges in rape cases "usually take into consideration the behavior of the victim prior to the time when the crime happened. Therefore a conviction is very difficult when the victim is a prostitute or had irregular behavior, even though the law does not make any distinction in that respect." They cite a case in which the court concluded that "it will not be necessary to cite the copious jurisprudence and the lesson of the value attributed to the word of the victim in crimes against custom when it is logical, plausible, coherent and comes from a woman of good moral background."[158]

While Brazilian judges may have a genuine interest in treating the proven crime of rape with severity, they are often influenced by misinformation about the nature of rape and hold prejudicial attitudes about rape victims which limit their ability to deliver equal justice.[159]

---

[156] Decision of the Superior Tribunal of Justice, March 1991.

[157] Attorney Linhares, interview with Americas Watch, April 1991.

[158] Fernandes and Marques, p. 273.

[159] Brazil is not alone in this regard. Information available about treatment of rape cases by the United States judiciary also indicates that discriminatory attitudes towards women influence the treatment of the crime. In testimony before the Senate Judiciary

As noted by Brazilian lawyer Silvia Pimentel, "under the law, rape doesn't demand for its configuration that the woman be honest. But the practice in rape cases, whether in the *delegacias* or the court, questions the personal history of the victim, though less so in the women's police stations. The question of whether a rape occurred ultimately rests on what type of victim the woman is."[160]

D. Marital Rape

By all accounts, marital rape is seriously under-reported in Brazil. A study of reported rapes in the state of Minas Gerais found that over half were perpetrated by strangers.[161] By contrast, data compiled by the U.S. Federal Bureau of Investigation indicate that over 60 percent of all reported rapes in the United States are committed by someone known to the victim.[162] Brazilian researchers were quick to point out that limited statistics regarding acquaintance or marital rape do not support the conclusion that such rape does not occur. They stressed that prevailing social and judicial attitudes that marital rape in particular is not a crime may substantially reduce reporting, police investigation and prosecution.

While marital rape is not widely reported in Brazil, a police chief in

---

Committee on April 9, 1991, Roland Burris, Attorney General for the State of Illinois, spoke of observing hearings in Illinois: "rather than a lack of awareness about the technical aspects of the law, it was *misinformation* about the nature of violent crimes directed at women and *erroneous personal beliefs* about the victims that were the major obstacles to achieving equal treatment under the law for women. One Chicago judge dismissed a rape case because the woman victim said that the attack took place at 10 a.m. The judge reasoned that no one would break into an apartment in the daylight with the shades up and risk being seen by the neighbors. Thus, he assumed the victim was lying." When making comparisons between the U.S. and Brazilian judiciary, it is important to underscore that the legal systems of the two countries are not the same. With regard to rape in particular, the legal definition differs and, in addition, rape in Brazil does not require a jury trial.

[160] Professor Silvia Pimentel, interview with Americas Watch, April 1991.

[161] da Conceição Marques Rubinger, Maria, et al, *Crimes Contra A Mulher: A Violência Denunciada*, table 17.

[162] Federal Bureau of Investigation, Uniform Crime Reports for the United States, Washington D.C., 1990, cited in *Violence Against Women As Bias Motivated Hate Crime*, Center for Women Policy Studies (Washington, D.C.: 1991), p. 4.

Belo Horizonte told Americas Watch that such abuses do occur. She told us of a marital rape registered at the *delegacia* on May 7, 1991:

> The woman's husband accused her of having sex with strangers. He then asked her to prove her love for him by having sex with strangers. He took her to nightclubs so that she could choose and seduce a stranger so that the three of them could have sex together.
>
> In one of several incidents between the couple, the husband took his wife to a dance club and he chose a partner and went to a hotel. The wife was forced to have sex with both men, vaginal, anal and oral. The IML's examinations confirmed the victim's version.

The *delegada* stressed that the victim herself did not report the sexual abuse by her husband until it became impossible for her to bear it any longer. Several activists, attorneys, police and judges with whom we spoke confirmed this pattern and noted that women may not recognize the treatment as criminal.

Anita, a child–care provider in the Santa Marta *favela* in Rio told Americas Watch that "women who are forced to have sex with their husbands feel it is an obligation. She feels violated in her person, but she feels it's her duty."[163] Cecília Soares, a civil attorney working in Rio with domestic–abuse cases, finds that for the women she represents, "What happens in marriage isn't considered a crime. Sex is an obligation of marriage. Marriage obliges her to have such relations. Women don't consider it rape, they don't consider it a crime."[164]

Although Brazilian law does not explicitly outlaw marital rape, the provisions relating to all forms of sexual abuse theoretically apply to violations which occur within a conjugal relation. However, under the Brazilian Civil Code, sexual relations are considered a marital obligation and refusal of sex is legal grounds for separation. According to Brazilian human rights lawyer Leila Linhares "when a husband uses violence it isn't seen as rape, but as defending conjugal rights." In practice, Brazilian judges generally reject the notion of marital rape. According to Linhares "some courts have understood that if violence or physical threat is used,

---

[163] Anita, interview with Americas Watch, April 1991.

[164] Cecília Soares, interview with Americas Watch, April 1991.

it is rape even if it is by the husband. But this is still not jurisprudence."[165]

E. Proposed Legal Reforms

For many Brazilian feminists, equal treatment of female rape victims by the criminal justice system would be greatly enhanced by a reform of the relevant criminal statutes. In 1988 the National Council on the Rights of Women under President Jacqueline Pitanguy held a National Forum of woman lawyers to discuss possible reforms following the passage of a new Constitution which enshrines equal rights for women. Constitutional lawyer Silvia Pimentel and several other Brazilian attorneys were nominated by the Forum to draft reforms which were later proposed to the Brazilian National Assembly. Their proposed reforms would eliminate the classification of rape as a Crime Against Custom and re-classify it under Title I as a Crime Against Persons.[166] This would have the double effect of highlighting rape as a crime against a human being and elevating it to an unconditional public-action crime, which mandates prosecution by the state.

They also propose combining Articles 213 and 214 of the Penal Code which deal with rape and anal and oral sex respectively. The drafters argue that the combination of these two articles would give the crime of rape "a comprehensive character" so that it would include not only forced vaginal sex, but also forced anal and oral sex. In addition, it would end the notion that only a woman can be a rape victim.

Finally, they proposed eliminating Penal Code provisions that criminalize certain acts only if they are committed against a "virgin" or "honest" woman. They proposed substituting more general provisions on "sexual abuse." The Forum also supported deleting the increase in penalty arising from a spousal relationship between the victim and accused. In the reformers' view, "there is no justification for stricter sentences for a married defendant....That presumes the admissibility of obsolete values."

---

165 Leila Linhares, interview with Americas Watch, April 1991. Marital rape was explicitly outlawed in Britain in 1991 and several, but not all, U.S. states have recently enacted prohibitions on marital rape as well.

166 *Proposta De Reformulação Dos Códigos Civil E Penal Brasileiros*, proposed by Forum Nacional de Presidentas de Conselhos e Secretarias da Condição e Direitos da Mulher, 1990. All following citations are from this document.

Professor Silvia Pimentel told Americas Watch that through these reforms the National Forum hopes to protect the individual rights of women, remove their legalized subordination to "custom" and guarantee rape victims of both sexes equal treatment under the law.

VI. OBSERVATIONS AND RECOMMENDATIONS

A. In General

Domestic violence can no longer be dismissed as a "private matter" in Brazil. It is a public and widespread problem which calls for an urgent government response. Yet, impunity and discriminatory treatment are still the rule. A man can kill his wife and be acquitted on the grounds of honor. A woman can be successfully accused of provoking a murder which was clearly premeditated so the defendant will receive a lighter sentence. Domestic battery and rape are rarely punished. Only a strong political commitment by the Brazilian government to end such discrimination can reverse this trend.

* We urge the Brazilian government to implement the law fully and fairly and uphold the right of equal protection for all its citizens regardless of sex.

* The Brazilian government should publicly denounce the legitimate defense of honor and propose the constitutional or statutory reforms necessary to ensure that the defense is no longer used. At a minimum, lower courts should be required to instruct juries that the defense of honor is not a legally recognized defense, to prevent defense attorneys from making such arguments and to refrain from asking juries to consider the defense.

* Judges should receive instruction on the narrow limits of the violent emotion defense and vigilance should be maintained to ensure that those limits are respected in practice.

* Judges and prosecutors should also receive instruction on the criminality of domestic abuse and the social prejudices which tolerate it. Judges in particular should be further reminded of their responsibility to uphold the law in the face of a jury verdict based on such prejudices which is against all material evidence.

B. Documentation of Violence Against Women

Efforts to improve the Brazilian government's response to domestic abuse would be greatly enhanced by the availability of reliable national data – broken down by gender – detailing the nature and degree of violence in the home. At present, national homicide figures by sex are not available and statistical information regarding battery and rape, while available through the *delegacias*, is usually compiled by hand and rarely in a systematic way. In the absence of reliable national statistics which accurately portray the seriousness of the domestic–violence problem, the Brazilian government is unlikely to develop an adequate response.

* We urge the Brazilian government to improve the collection of data concerning crimes of violence against women. We recommend that the government first conduct a review of all existing statistical information on domestic violence in the country. Such a review should include, at a minimum, the incidence of such violence, rates of prosecution and severity of punishment. With the aid of these findings, a system for improved collection and dissemination of national data on violence against women should be designed, including an active role for the *delegacias*.

C. Police Training

The women's *delegacias* are on the front line of efforts to criminalize domestic abuse. They are one of the Brazilian government's most effective resources in this area. Yet they have been prohibited from investigating homicide, one of the most serious crimes of violence against women, and their work has been hampered by the absence of consistent state and national support, by a lack of qualified personnel and, perhaps most important, by lack of training.

* The Brazilian government should enable and fully prepare the women's police stations to investigate murders in which the victim is a female.

* The Brazilian government should support the women's *delegacias* by making resources available for their expansion throughout the country. Such an effort should be undertaken in cooperation with state and municipal authorities to ensure adequate economic and political support and effective geographic distribution.

* A training program on domestic violence should be introduced in all police academies. Individuals or institutions with expertise in this area should be commissioned by the government to develop such a program and should work together with the relevant authorities to effect its implementation on a national scale.

D. The Medical–Legal System

Brazilian law provides that any woman registering a crime of physical or sexual abuse with the police must visit the Medical–Legal Institute (IML) for a medical examination. Yet the IMLs are centralized in urban areas beyond the reach of many women, and lack female personnel trained in forensic medicine as well as specialists trained in violent sexual crimes. The result can often be demeaning and inaccurate medical exams which omit vital medical–legal proof and pose a serious disincentive to women victims of physical or sexual abuse, who may already be hesitant to report such incidents, from proceeding with prosecution.

* The Brazilian government should take the necessary steps to enable medical facilities other than the IML, including licensed private physicians, to give testimony and introduce physical evidence in court regarding the degree and nature of physical and sexual abuse.

* The IML facilities should be decentralized and female physicians recruited and trained in forensic medicine. Each IML should also be staffed with specialists trained in the physical and psychological effects of violent sexual abuse.

E. Legal Reform

The Brazilian government's ratification of the Convention on the Elimination of All Forms of Discrimination Against Women (CEDAW) represents a major commitment to outlaw discrimination against women in Brazil in all its forms. However, the Brazilian government's failure to satisfy its reporting obligations under CEDAW calls into question the seriousness of its commitment to the principle of non–discrimination.

The 1988 Brazilian Constitution contains model women's rights provisions. However, Penal and Civil Code reforms needed to implement those principles have yet to be enacted.

* The Brazilian government should, as required by Article 18 of CEDAW, submit to the Secretary General of the United Nations for consideration by the committee which oversees the Convention a report on the legislative, judicial, administrative and other measures which it has taken to give effect to the Convention's provisions.

* The Brazilian government should propose to the National Assembly reforms of the Civil and Penal Codes guaranteeing the implementation of principles set out in the Constitution relating to women, particularly those concerning women's status in the home, the abolition of adultery as a crime and the reclassification and redefinition of sex crimes.

F. Legal and Social Aid

A female victim who seeks to pursue criminal prosecution of a crime of domestic violence may have limited knowledge of her legal rights and lack adequate representation. This will seriously reduce her access to justice.

Because there is only one public shelter operating in all of Brazil, with the possibility of two more opening, women who pursue criminal prosecution routinely find themselves with no alternative but to return home. This can pose extreme personal risk to the victim as well as discourage her from seeking justice.

* The provision of free legal assistance to indigent women victims of domestic violence should be increased, particularly those who seek to prosecute domestic violence crimes.

* National and state authorities should provide funds for public shelters for victims of domestic violence and their dependant children.

Human Rights Watch

Human Rights Watch is composed of Africa Watch, Americas Watch, Asia Watch, Helsinki Watch and Middle East Watch, and the Fund for Free Expression.

Addresses for Human Rights Watch and its Divisions

485 Fifth Avenue
New York, NY 10017
Tel: (212) 972-8400
Fax: (212) 972-0905

1522 K Street, NW, Suite 910
Washington, DC 20005
Tel: (202) 371-6592
Fax: (202) 371-0124

10951 West Pico Blvd., #203
Los Angeles, CA 90064
Tel: (213) 475-3070
Fax: (213) 475-5613

90 Borough High Street
London SEI ILL, UK
Tel: (071) 378-8008
Fax: (071) 378-8029